Ladies First

Ladies First

Women in
Music Videos

Robin Roberts

University Press of Mississippi   Jackson

Some of the arguments in chapter 1 appeared in "'Sex as a Weapon': Feminist Rock Music Videos," in *National Women's Studies Association Journal* 2 (1990):1–15. A portion of chapter 2 was published as "Humor and Gender in Music Videos," in *Sexual Politics and Popular Culture*, edited by Diane Raymond (Bowling Green: Popular Press, 1990), 173–82. Earlier versions of chapter 6 were published as "Music Videos, Performance, and Resistance: Feminist Rappers," in *Journal of Popular Culture* 25 (1991): 141–52, and "Sisters in the Name of Rap: Rapping for Women's Lives," in *Black Women in America*, edited by Kim Marie Vaz (Menlo Park, CA: Sage Publications, 1994), 323–33. Chapter 7 appeared in an earlier form as "Ladies First: Queen Latifah's Afrocentric Feminist Music Video," in *African American Review* 28, no. 2 (1994): 245–57.

Print-on-Demand Edition

The paper in this book meets the guidelines for permanence and durability of the Committee on Production Guidelines for Book Longevity of the Council on Library Resources.

Library of Congress Cataloging-in-Publication Data

Roberts, Robin, 1957–
    Ladies first : women in music videos / Robin Roberts.
      p. cm.
    Videography: p.
    Includes bibliographical references (p.   ) and index.

    ISBN 978-1-60473-397-6

    1. Feminism and music.   2. Music videos—Social aspects—United States.
ML82.R63   1996
781.64'082—dc20   96-14969
                                  CIP
                                 MN

British Library Cataloging-in-Publication data available

To Nina Auerbach—teacher, mentor, role model

Contents

ACKNOWLEDGMENTS   ix

INTRODUCTION   xi

1. "SEX AS A WEAPON": FEMINISM, POSTMODERNISM AND MUSIC VIDEOS   3

2. "THE HOMECOMING QUEEN'S GOT A GUN": HUMOR AND GENDER IN FEMINIST MUSIC VIDEOS   32

3. "JUSTIFY MY LOVE": MUSIC VIDEOS AND THE CONSTRUCTION OF SEXUALITY   59

4. "ALTERNATIVE NATION": ALTERNATIVE MUSIC, FEMINISM AND *BEAVIS AND BUTT-HEAD*   81

5. "INDEPENDENCE DAY": FEMINIST COUNTRY MUSIC VIDEOS   110

6. "SISTERS IN THE NAME OF RAP": FEMINIST RAP MUSIC VIDEOS   138

7. "LADIES FIRST": QUEEN LATIFAH'S AFROCENTRIC VIDEO   163

NOTES   185

WORKS CITED   191

VIDEOGRAPHY   203

INDEX   205

Acknowledgments

I am grateful to Lisa A. Lewis, whose ground-breaking scholarship has been an inspiration, and whose comments on earlier versions improved the book considerably. Seetha A-Srinivasan, my editor at the University Press of Mississippi, saw the possibilities in this work and provided invaluable encouragement. I am grateful to Daniel Fogel, Associate Vice-Chancellor and Dean of the graduate school at LSU for his support. Dean Karl Roider and Associate Dean Craig Cordes also provided assistance. LSU Academic Affairs and the College of Arts & Sciences generously gave funds for copyright permissions. My thanks go to Carol Cox for her careful copy-editing. Carol Mattingly and Maggie Mudd shared their perceptive insights into popular culture, and Carol's encouragement was crucial. Emily and Bruce Toth helped by believing in and liking *Beavis and Butt-Head* (though Emily still prefers Beavis). Frank de Caro and Rosan Jordan showed me the delights of country music. I thank Rachel Kahn, Kevin Wong, Sharon Weltman, Randall Knoper, Pat Day, Elsie Michie, Carl Freedman, Susan Kohler, and Julie de Sherbinin. Lucy, Tom, Bobcat, and Darcy all helped, too. Special thanks go to Peter Fischer, who asked me to justify my analysis, and to Keith Kelleman, who was there when MTV began. Shirley, Gayle, and Linda Roberts gave much-needed support, even if they did think I should write a novel instead. Louisiana State University provided a sabbatical that enabled me to complete this work, and all my students at Lafayette College, Colby College, and

LSU contributed to this book. They were my first and best audience.

Introduction

Music videos emphasize the construction of the self; in myriad ways, a music video reveals the construction of a variety of personae by the performer. The creation of a marketable self has been a primary reason for the production of music videos by record companies and performers. The promotional aspect of music videos determines their form, but feminist music videos show that even advertising, which has long been singled out as a source of misogynist and sexist depictions of women, can be turned to a feminist end.

Music videos primarily function as advertisements for albums and tours. All videos on MTV, VH-1, The Nashville Network, Country Music Television and Black Entertainment Television display song title, album title, artist's name, and record label—information needed to buy a compact disc (CD) or cassette. Usually, these channels do not provide information about video directors or other credits that we expect in a film (only recently, for some videos, has MTV begun to identify the director, and even then the information is the last given in a series that begins with the performer's name). In addition, music video collections are marketed and sold under the artist's name. Marsha Kinder explains that "*everything* on MTV is a commercial—advertising spots, news, station ID's, interviews, and especially music video clips" (5). Like other advertisements, music videos often use women's bodies to sell the product—in this case a compact disc or a cassette. Because of the blatantly promotional nature of music videos, most discussion tends to focus on this function and on the effect of the commodifying cycle on the video. As E. Ann Kaplan notes, "There is a built-in contradiction, familiar from Hollywood, between the interests of the artists and performers, and of those creating a profitable enterprise" (1987, 147). In the typical Marxist analysis, such as those that dominate Donald Lazere's *American Media and Mass Culture,* the artist loses to the power of capital.

Paradoxically, it is this very quality of promotion that some women artists are beginning to exploit for feminist ends. On a basic level, promotion in music videos involves the self-promotion of the artist as a desirable or admirable image. If the product being promoted is a strong female image, the music video can then potentially be used for a feminist purpose. The texts discussed in this book provide examples of such subversions. These music videos confirm Michel Foucault's assertion that "power is exercised from innumerable points, in the interplay of nonegalitarian and mobile relations" (1976, 94). If not an unalloyed good, this use of capitalist structures provides, at least, a sign of possibilities for play and potential for movement. Market forces do not necessarily or inevitably operate against feminism. For example, in response to the competition offered by other music video shows and channels, in 1985 MTV decided to pay for some videos in return for exclusive rights. One of these videos was the explicitly feminist "Sisters Are Doing It for Themselves," performed by Annie Lennox and Aretha Franklin. Because it was created and has prospered as a promotional channel, MTV has been and will continue to be responsive to market forces. But the commercial aspects of MTV decried by some of its critics may prove its redemption. Although the channel reacts slowly, it does respond to criticism and competition. One competitor, U 68,[1] showed music videos by less mainstream rock groups, even by groups who had only put out singles on minor labels, and MTV responded by altering its standards to include such videos, specifically those by women and blacks. In fact, a recent study suggests that music videos are a particularly potent form of social construction for women and minorities; according to this study, women and blacks watch more music videos than other groups of teenagers (Brown, Campbell, and Fischer, 19–32).

Female performers and female audiences have been increasing at the same time that women are achieving more power in music companies. While there are few studies on female music executives, those that exist suggest that there is new power and visibility for women executives in the music industry. In the late 1980s and early 1990s, articles in *Billboard*, the music industry's journal of record, show an attention to the number and concerns of women music executives. The New Music Seminar, an important conference, held a panel entitled "Sexism in the Music Industry" in 1989 (McDonnell). While this panel and a number of articles describe the music industry as an old boys' network that still needs to change, the existence of nine panelists with executive jobs in the music industry reflects significant change already. Before the 1980s, women were almost exclusively secretarial staff or in publicity rather than holding the more prestigious and important "artist and repertoire" or management positions. In 1990 G. Mayfield reported that "if you scan the rosters of label sales divisions and distribution networks, there are more women and blacks in key positions than there were 10, or even five years ago" (40).

In a 1988 study, Patrick R. Parsons explains that there have been no previous studies of women executives in the music industry because there were no women to study. He also notes how the music industry concentrates a great deal of power in a few hands (31), so that even a few women in key positions can wield tremendous influence. His study reveals that the proportion of women executives in the music business rose from 5 percent in 1966 to 32 percent in 1988, with a decrease in the number of women in publicity and promotion (37). He describes "an increasing influx of women into management positions" (40). In her study of women in rock and roll, *She's A Rebel*, Gillian G. Gaar briefly cites the same phenomenon, quoting a woman executive as saying that "there's a smattering of female vice presidents. And each year there's more. I think things are changing now" (354). Significantly, Parsons also identifies music videos as an area of the music industry more open to women (37). He concludes with a call for more research, but even his limited study shows that music videos are helpful for women executives as well as for the women performers who are the focus of this book.

Music videos are a new cultural form that requires more of its viewers. Feminist music videos provide an example of what John Fiske calls the "producerly" text. He identifies this text as being situated between Roland Barthes's "readerly" text, which relies on a passive, receptive reader, and a "writerly" text, which challenges the reader to rewrite the text to make sense of it (103–104). Music videos are more like a writerly text in that they are open to interpretation and, in fact, require some effort on the part of the viewer; at the same time, they are not as difficult or as abstruse as a truly writerly text. In short, music videos are accessible but involve some production on the part of the viewer. They have, as Fiske claims for other popular culture texts, the best of both worlds.

As a genre, music videos resist traditional categorization and analysis. Even music videophobes like Sut Jhally, a communications professor at the University of Massachusetts, acknowledge that the form itself demands a new kind of analysis. In his critique of the sexism and racism of music videos, Jhally makes his case by producing a video, *Dreamworlds*, that shows images but has no music. This sundering draws attention to the complexity of music videos as a text, illustrating how they communicate on at least three levels: that of the music, that of the images, and that of the two together. *Ladies First*, by contrast, insists that all three levels must be considered, and, for this reason, a videotape of the music videos is included with the text. It is my hope that readers will consume the two together, and discover, as I have, pleasure in women music video performers. Since the feminist music videotape includes rock and roll, country music, and rap, viewers will find new ways of looking at genres they are familiar with, as well as new genres to enjoy.

A Marxist approach like Jhally's seems quite outdated when placed in the context of a postmodern approach to music videos as texts. To appreciate these new forms, feminists must open new channels of inquiry. While some feminist critics, including Angela McRobbie and Emily Toth, advocate a positive feminist exploration of popular culture, others see popular culture as a site of oppression. For example, in 1991, *On the Issues: The Progressive Woman's Quarterly* had a lead story entitled "The Dangerous Misogyny of MTV," and Susan Faludi's bestselling *Backlash* trenchantly criticizes popular film. At the National Women's Studies Association, where I have presented papers on music videos for the past several years, I am invariably criticized by a member of the audience who refuses, for feminist reasons, to watch MTV. The emphasis in earlier feminist criticism on the ways in which popular culture abuses and degrades women has demonstrated the harm in dominant representations of women in popular culture, especially in the world of rock and roll. This world, however, also offers moments of resistance to such abusive stereotyping. While such resistance is now widely recognized, it still must be argued within certain feminist contexts. I do not mean to suggest that feminists should embrace all of popular culture but rather that some forms of popular culture, especially music videos, should be considered legitimate and crucial sites of feminist inquiry.

In her otherwise insightful and compelling book on music videos, *Rocking Around the Clock: Music Television, Postmodernism, and Consumer Culture* (1987), E. Ann Kaplan falls into the trap of dismissing the more positive depictions of and by women. Her pessimism is part of a postmodernist cynicism about resistance. Providing a thorough schematic overview of the types of music videos, Kaplan briefly discusses feminist music videos, but refers to them as "so-called 'feminist' videos" (88). While acknowledging the possibility of resistance, she dismisses it almost immediately. Furthermore, this pioneering work is in need of revision; since its publication, new types of feminist music videos have emerged. Country music and rap music videos are recent developments. Criticism of music videos must continue to develop along with the genre.

Ladies First both continues the discussion of music videos begun by Kaplan and develops Lisa A. Lewis's brilliant analyses of gender in music videos, *Gender Politics and MTV: Voicing the Difference* (1990). Lewis's contribution lies in her careful attention to gender in the consumption of music videos. Unlike any other music video critic, Lewis carefully considers the role of the fan. She treats at length the question of resistance to gender stereotypes in music videos. Her discussion of fan culture and her biographies of prominent female performers Tina Turner, Pat Benatar, Cyndi Lauper and Madonna provide vivid examples of feminist resistance in a genre that had, as she points out, been unfairly depicted as monolithic. While Lewis's book explores fans and fan culture, *Ladies First* expands the notion of performance to include a wide range of music video types. Where Lewis privileges performers and *their* texts, *Ladies First* considers both, emphasizing the music video text. A star-centered approach is certainly justified by the star-centered nature of music videos, but highlighting music videos by genre and theme reveals important concerns not central to Lewis's thesis. And while Lewis considers that the emphasis on textual inquiry limits the discussion of music videos to the exposure of oppression, the analysis of texts in *Ladies First* demonstrates that the resistance she identifies as occurring in fan culture appears *within* genres as well.

In *Ladies First*, I examine music videos to discover how, even in an arena so overtly misogynist and commercial, resistance to dominant cultural practices occurs. As a feminist cultural critic influenced by poststructuralism,

I expected to find some resistance, because poststructuralist theorists from Jacques Derrida to Jean-François Lyotard have shown that no system or narrative is monolithic. Looking at narratives as multivocal requires the acknowledgment, always, of at least the possibility of resistance, for a text never speaks in a single, unified, uncontradictory voice. Instead, there are various performances in any text. Lyotard, for example, stresses the importance of performativity in narrative when he explains that "[i]t tends to jolt everyday discourse into a kind of metadiscourse: ordinary statements are now displaying a propensity for self-citation" (62). Lyotard is referring to scientific narrative, but his description applies as well to music videos, which in their commercial function have become part of everyday discourse, but which, when examined, reveal discourse about discourse and self-referentiality.

Textual performance in music videos deserves feminist inquiry, for performativity is important not only to theorists like Lyotard but also to theorists of gender like Judith Butler, whose *Gender Trouble* is subtitled *Feminism and the Subversion of Identity*. Acknowledging the performative aspects of gender roles allows Butler to foreground the subversive aspects of gender formation. Similarly, acknowledging the performative aspects of gender enables my reading of resistance in music videos. Looking at music videos from a poststructuralist view allows us to see the ways in which postmodern qualities and our postmodern culture provide opportunities for women. Poststructuralism licenses the reading of the body and performance as legitimate texts, and allows us to look beyond traditional sexist notions of authorship to see that female performers are also authors of the video texts.

Like Butler's, my approach to popular culture texts such as music videos builds on this understanding of the construction of femininity. Not only feminist theorists but also female performers provide clues and critiques of the construction of femininity through both their words and their performances. This reification of the role of performers is partly what undergirds *Ladies First*'s feminism: I take female performers seriously as agents. In this regard I associate my feminism with that of the performers; like them, I am hopeful about the possibility of action by women. *Ladies First* highlights the achievements of women performers and their use of postmodernism to create strategies of resistance. Instead of an earlier feminist vision of alternative artistic practice, music videos provide an example of intervention, engagement and disruption that echoes the work of high artists like Jenny Holzer, whose "feminine sentences" have appeared on marquees in Times Square and other similarly public arenas.

Indeed, a pivotal moment in the development of MTV occurred when the channel began incorporating the work of Jenny Holzer and other postmodern artists in a program entitled *Buzz*. (This alternative programming still exists in *Buzz Clips*, which shows music videos that have innovative visual and musical elements.) I single out Holzer's work because hers is the most overtly feminist. It was undoubtedly Holzer's high-art credentials and her use of electronic media that made her suited for MTV— after all, her work frequently appears in other high-visibility, high-tech venues. With her postmodern ethos, she was appropriate for MTV, and her feminist message gained an enormous mass-market outlet.

In a segment that aired in 1989, Holzer explains her art in a voice-over as the camera pans several installations, settling last on "MEN DON'T PROTECT YOU ANYMORE" in flashing red letters on an unidentified marquee looming over a city street. The statement has clear feminist implications about such matters as chivalry and gender relations. More important than the specific content, however, is Holzer's explanation of what she is doing, for it applies as well to the feminist music videos that also air on MTV. "I use the electronic signs," she explains in the voice-over, "because they seem like the medium of Big Brother, but then I put surprising and peculiar content that puts a certain twist on things." Similarly, feminist music videos air on MTV, which seems like the medium, if not of the political Big Brother, at least of the patriarchal Big Brother. But, as the music videos discussed in this book demonstrate, women performers are able to put a surprising and peculiar twist on gender relations. Holzer also expresses the desire to have viewers "be a little more aware of what goes on around them . . . possibly even figure out what to do." Holzer has been described as arriving "at her distinctive use of language at a time when narrative art was being born of conceptualism via feminism" (Princenthal 32). It is this combination of postmodernism and feminism that characterizes the feminist texts on MTV, and Holzer's modest but clearly expressed desire to destabilize is part of the postmodern position of many feminist music video performers.

Feminist music videos embody Janet Wolff's description of resistant art: "By employing the much-cited postmodern tactics of pastiche, irony, quotation, and juxtaposition, this kind of cultural politics engages directly with current images, forms, and ideas, subverting their intent and (re)appropriating their meanings, rather than abandoning them for alternative forms, which would leave them untouched and still dominant" (88). *Ladies First* shows that feminist music videos provide an appropriate and compelling resistance through fragmentation and complication of the dominant music video ethos. The first chapter provides a concrete example of why and how postmodernism can be helpful to feminists and to critics of music videos, thus refuting Andrew Goodwin's simplistic blanket condemnation of the use of postmodernism in the discussion of music videos (15, 176).

Postmodernist qualities can be used to shake up traditional images of gender; not only music videos but MTV itself deals with gender transgressions in a playful, postmodern manner. For example, an MTV channel identification that first aired in 1994 emphasizes the idea of playing with gender role reversals. In a series of cartoon frames, Clark Kent and Lois Lane look-alikes confront a masked gunman who threatens them. "Oh, John," the female figure exclaims, and then, as John cringes back, his shirt opening to reveal a bra, Jane bursts her shirt to display an MTV/Superwoman logo. She vanquishes the attacker. While this station identification has a practical function, it is also an illustration of MTV's providing space for playing with traditional gender roles. Using a postmodern reference to comics and the Superman television series, the identification points out the changes that have occurred in the representations of femininity and masculinity. This playfulness and use of animation appear in many feminist music videos. The station identification is also postmodern in its emphasis on narrative as performance. The action all takes place bordered by a frame that is reminiscent of the Sunday comics. This identification reveals many of the features that appear in feminist music videos and also in the MTV show *Beavis and Butt-Head* (discussed in chapter 4). Considering music videos as a special type of postmodern narrative helps us to understand how their postmodern form enables a feminist message about the construction and performance of gender.

Ladies First examines a wider range of feminist music videos than have previous books on music videos. Further, this book focuses on a range of music videos as texts rather than emphasizing the institution of MTV itself. Kaplan, R. Serge Denisoff and others concentrate primarily or even exclusively on MTV. While attention to MTV is certainly merited because the channel has so dominated music videos, especially in the 1980s, there are now numerous music video shows and channels. Emphasizing MTV gives it a singular prominence that is not warranted in the 1990s when the channel itself now stresses cartoons, comedy shows, sports shows, and other nonmusical programming. Moving from an exclusive analysis of MTV acknowledges the development of other venues for music video performers, some of which, like Black Entertainment Television's *Rap City*, prove to be more amenable to feminist performances.

The culture industries of the 1990s are very different from those of the 1970s or even the 1980s, and music video channels reflect the new importance of women performers, audiences, and producers. Country Music Television, The Nashville Network, VH-1, MTV, and Black Entertainment Television all reflect the acceptance of women performers and female audiences. *Ladies First* explores the texts that reflect this cultural shift. By focusing on feminist music videos from the mid-1980s to the mid-1990s, this book captures a slice of popular culture history that reveals the progression of feminist performers' use of postmodernism.

The use of the word "feminist" in the term "feminist music videos" in this book is complicated. In general, I argue that music videos by some female performers communicate "feminist messages," that is, messages about issues of concern to women that have been connected to "second wave" feminism: sexual harassment, domestic violence, unequal relationships, feminine sexual desire, the social construction of femininity. Interviews with the female performers considered here reveal some ambivalence about the descriptor "feminist." Some performers, like rappers Salt 'n Pepa, acknowledge it, saying, "We're feminists" (Gaar 424), while others, like country music performer Trisha Yearwood, declare that they are "not card-carrying feminists" (Kingsbury 1992a, 18). What seems more important than an active membership in the National Organization for Women or self-identification as a feminist is the visual and lyrical content of the music video and the persona of the performer. As a literary critic, I look for textual evidence of feminist issues and signs. The close readings of the music videos I discuss provide the evidence for their feminism, which is by no means rigid among performers and genres. Yet all the music videos discussed in this book communicate a "feminist message," defined by Joan Radner and Susan Lanser as being "messages critical of some aspects of women's subordination" (3). Through their characterizations of themselves as strong, powerful, active women, the performers in a certain sense "perform" feminism. They can be said to model feminism for their viewers.

There are some compelling recurring motifs and themes that run through feminist music videos. The dozen or so videos discussed here are representative and do not constitute a list of the few feminist music videos. The music videos I have selected represent a wide time period, from 1985 to 1994, and they cover genres as diverse as country music and rap. Yet despite these differences, we find repeated references to Cinderella and Cleopatra as problematic and emblematic female figures. As with female literary traditions, female music video performers draw on narratives and figures that address the matter of women's position in society. This intertextuality is what makes feminist music videos worth studying and teaching, not only individually but also as a group. It is my hope that the reader of this book will feel inspired to explore the many music video outlets and to use music videos, as I have, to raise feminist issues in the classroom and in other venues. Most of all, I hope to introduce the reader to feminist success stories and to the pleasure of consuming music videos with female performers.

This book is divided into two parts. The first half, chapters 1 through 3, explores theoretical areas that are central to a discussion of feminism and music videos—postmodernism, humor, and sexuality—and explains their significance for feminist music video performance. The second half, chapters 4 through 7, examines feminist music videos in specific musical genres (alternative music, country music, rap), and shows how postmodernism, humor and sexuality are used by female performers to produce specific generic qualities that create feminist messages.

The first chapter, " 'Sex as Weapon': Feminism, Postmodernism and Music Videos," identifies the central question about postmodernism and feminism: how can the deconstructive possibilities of the postmodern art form be harnessed for the subversive agenda of a feminism committed to questioning the traditional limited role of femininity? This chapter discusses music videos' postmodern qualities and demonstrates ways in which style can be used against hegemonic discourse and how form can co-opt a dominant discourse—in this case, the discourse of patriarchy. E. Ann Kaplan acknowledges that "even in the commercial postmodernism exemplified in MTV, . . . there are benefits for the female spectator: the breaking up of traditional realist forms sometimes entails a deconstruction of conventional sex-role representations that opens up new possibilities for female imagining" (1988, 39).

Poststructuralist theory produces a new understanding of narrative in which a "text" is freed from monologic and auteurist assumptions. The author of a multivoiced music video is not only the (typically male) director but also the performer who interweaves meanings through her delivery, look, gestures, and, in many cases, music and lyrics. As Steven Connor says, "The aesthetic that emerges from this is . . . simulated authorship, in which ideas of originality and repetition, authenticity and theft, are teased out to their problematic limits" (95). This emphasis on tension and on multiple participants rather than on a single author promotes resistance to the controlling interests of one ideology. The female performer, then, can be discussed as an author of the text.

What Connor writes about postmodernist literary authors applies to music video performers: in their work, "the 'post' of postmodernism signifies not the fatigue of the late-comer, but the freedom and self-assertion of those who have awoken from the past" (65). Acknowledging a variety of nondirectorial influences allows for resistance in subtle forms, permitting me a perspective that emphasizes the radical possibilities of postmodern art forms.

Chapter 2, "'The Homecoming Queen's Got a Gun': Humor and Gender in Feminist Music Videos," identifies resistance to traditional gender roles through use of one of the oldest forms of subversion and criticism, humor. In this chapter, I rely on new theories about women's humor to explain the humorous music video. An anthology of criticism entitled *Last Laughs: Perspectives on Women and Comedy* repeatedly makes the point that women's humor is aggressive, disturbing, and disruptive; the editor, Regina Barreca, explains that "women's comedy is marginal, liminal, concerned with and defined by its very exclusion from convention, by its aspects of refusal and its alliance with subversive feminine symbols. The difference of women is viewed as a risk to culture. So it should be" (15). Julie Brown's "The Homecoming Queen's Got a Gun" typifies this description, for Brown's video was initially banned from MTV for being "too violent," even though the video depicts no realistic violence. What the humorous music video does do, however, is to make fun of traditional feminine roles. Music video performers draw on the postmodern form and the idea that sexuality can be constructed to ridicule gender stereotyping. Taking humor seriously as a form of resistance enables the viewer to see how such a strategy can be utilized by a subordinate group like women, an issue that is increasingly the focus of humor studies.

Chapter 3, "'Justify Your Love': Music Videos and the Construction of Sexuality," explores how music videos participate in the construction of sexuality. Music videos simultaneously reinforce traditional constructions of sexuality and reject the dominant discourse by presenting moments of resistance. In this chapter, I discuss concerns about the visual depictions of women and female sexuality in music videos in such a way as to clarify the debates about pornography, sexuality and representation. Historically, sexuality was seen as a source of danger for women. The conflict between feminists who envision an open expression and acceptance of all types of sexuality and those who oppose pornographic depictions of women has a central place in the discussion of music videos. My own experiences in being accosted by those who dismiss all music videos as pornographic and who claim that no feminist should dignify music videos by studying them attests to such importance. While there certainly are music videos that draw on demeaning and degrading images of women, to thus dismiss the genre would be the equivalent of dismissing photography simply because photographs are a frequent site of pornographic images. In an effort to clarify such debates, this chapter explores the complex and contradictory presentation of sexuality by En Vogue and Madonna.

Chapter 4, "'Alternative Nation': Alternative Music, Feminism and *Beavis and Butt-Head*," turns the study from themes to genres. Here I explore "alternative music." Alternative music's receptivity to female performers and its characteristic resistance to traditional social mores make it especially suitable for feminist appropriation. This chapter explores "Miss World," written and performed by Hole, fronted by Courtney Love, and "If That's Your Boyfriend (He Wasn't Last Night)," written and performed by Me'shell NdegeOcello. Finally, the chapter turns to *Beavis and Butt-Head*, the tremendously popular show on MTV featuring the eponymous characters watching and commenting on music videos (especially alternative music videos), and reveals that the program uses a postmodern style to raise feminist issues.

Chapter 5, "'Independence Day': Feminist Country Music Videos," analyzes the development of feminist country music videos. Country music can no longer be seen or dismissed as a marginal or regional genre, since its popularity has increased dramatically. The generalizations made to explain country music's popularity, however, do not necessarily apply to the extremely successful women performers. Although Susan Holly writes, "The popular wisdom is that Americans are turning back to hearth and home for comfort in sober economic times" (34), such an explanation does not acknowledge the radical critiques of hearth and home made by female country music performers. This chapter and the two subsequent ones on rap provide examples of feminist performances in genres traditionally considered sexist.

Chapter 6, "'Sisters in the Name of Rap': Feminist Rap Music Videos," focuses on performers who draw on rap specifically as an African-American art form to resist racism, drawing additional energy from their simultaneous discussion of race and gender. This coupling enables women performers to attack discrimination more effectively. The dynamic of rap also requires that the performer focus on personal narrative, which, in the hands of a woman rapper, can mean a feminist tale.

Female rappers compete with male performers and gain attention for their feminist message through music videos. As a result of their perspective—they are both part of the rap scene and opponents to its misogyny—African-American female performers have a paradoxically strong position as both insiders and outsiders in this art form. This chapter emphasizes the issues of postmodernism and feminism with which the book begins. Rap's postmodernist qualities have been ignored, perhaps because postmodernism is usually associated with white, "high," masculine culture. Rap is only now beginning to receive critical attention, but, not surprisingly, several recent books on rap (Spencer; Toop; Costello and Wallace; Baker) neglect the contributions of female rappers and none discusses music videos. And, while two feminist critics, Tricia Rose and Cheryl Keyes, write about female rappers, again the music videos are not a central part of their analysis.

The final chapter, " 'Ladies First': Queen Latifah's Afrocentric Video," demonstrates that a feminist music video can sustain an extended textual analysis. I examine lyrics, images, and their combination to make an explicit and compelling challenge to hegemonic constructions of African-American women. Feminist music videos merit our attention both as a subgroup of the music video genre and as individual texts that are sophisticated and complex enough to demand close readings.

Ladies First

Chapter One

"Sex as a Weapon": Feminism, Postmodernism and Music Videos

Even in the commercial postmodernism exemplified in MTV . . . there are benefits for the female spectator.   —E. Ann Kaplan

Music videos provide an ideal site for an exploration of the issues raised by the conjunction of postmodernism and feminism. Widely criticized as being apolitical, postmodernism does provide the opportunity for politically progressive representations of a feminist politics. In a broad range of popular music genres, including country music, rock and roll, and rap, female performers use a postmodern art form, the music video, to communicate a feminist view. Especially through the vehicle of music videos, culture industries in the 1990s promulgate "feminist messages" (Radner 3), that is, messages that identify and comment on issues considered feminist, such as sexual harassment and domestic violence. A full understanding of the feminist messages that appear in this postmodern art form, the music video, requires some exploration of the theoretical linkage of feminism and postmodernism. This chapter's discussion of music videos provides an opportunity to see postmodernist categories, which are so often mystified in theoretical articles, used and manipulated.

Whether the amorphous entities of feminism and postmodernism should be linked at all seems no longer to be in question, according to a number of books, including Chris Weedon's *Feminist Practice and Poststructuralist Theory* (1987), Linda Nicholson's edited collection *Feminism/Postmodernism* (1990), and Angela McRobbie's *Postmodernism and Popular Culture* (1994), among others. Linda Singer writes that "at this historical moment [1992], feminism and postmodernism seems to be a relatively 'hot,' marketable duo" (472).

Yet for some feminists, postmodernism is "threatening . . . because it radically changes [their] background assumptions and contexts" (Flax 1992, 446). And feminists seem far more interested in appropriating postmodernism than postmodernism seems to be in drawing on feminism. Feminism and postmodernism can be seen as contradictory in part because they serve parallel, but apparently separate, functions.

Feminism and postmodernism can be described as simultaneously having a set of formal characteristics and being a social condition. Certain theorists emphasize one approach or the other, but both pertain to this discussion of music videos. Feminist music videos reveal formal features as well as a social context that frames how we interpret those features. Feminism can be defined as the movement for the social, political and economic equality of women, and it is as well a mindset and a value system. Postmodernism's list of qualities includes fragmentation, especially of subjectivity; a breakdown between the fine arts, the avant-garde, and the mass media; an emphasis on pastiche; repeated self-reflexiveness; and a challenge to the belief in master narratives. Postmodernism, too, can be considered a mindset, and it contains an implicit value system. The word "postmodernism" is used here according to its original application—to describe an art form. In the 1950s, the term was coined to identify a new form of architecture that was marked by an eclectic combination of composed styles; it has since been expanded to apply to almost any cultural manifestation, including theories about culture. In this book, the term "postmodernism" is used only to discuss art forms and culture, while the term "poststructuralism" is used to identify a body of theories about postmodern culture.

Jean-François Lyotard crucially identifies the postmodern as a "condition," and stresses that it is characterized by a breakdown of "grand narratives." Lyotard's emphasis on postmodernism as lived experience makes it a more ubiquitous and powerful phenomenon than if it were merely an abstract set of aesthetic qualities. We can no longer believe, uncritically, in the stories of science, including notions of progress and justification. No one system holds up any longer to a postmodern destabilizing. And, of course, while Lyotard focuses on science, a feminist reading *The Postmodern Condition* will immediately be able to identify patriarchy as a "grand narrative" that is losing its efficacy.

Postmodern art, like poststructuralist theory, stresses paradox, contradiction, and self-awareness. These elements lend themselves to the deconstruction of gender. In fact, many critics argue that feminist theory, because of its undermining aims, is closely related to postmodern theory. "As a type of postmodern philosophy, feminist theory reveals and contributes to the growing uncertainty within Western intellectual circles about the appropriate grounding and methods for explaining and/or interpreting human experience," Jane Flax explains (1990, 40–41). Until recently, however, feminist criticism and postmodern theory have developed in parallel lines, without intersecting.

Yet both feminism and postmodernism have been treated with suspicion by conservative forces. Both have been represented as tearing down traditional values and the patriarchal social structure. As Linda Singer explains, "Both feminism and postmodernism have been subjected in recent years to conservative reductionist critiques, which operate by constructing each as a monolithic dogmatic discourse, opaque to outsiders, organized by arcane rhetoric and rituals from within" (474). Similar attacks are not all that connect postmodernism and feminism. Postmodern style lends itself well to disruptions of old patterns and creation of new forms that can be used by feminists.

A number of feminist critics draw upon postmodern theory in their work. Chris Weedon, Linda Nicholson, and Angela McRobbie have made important contributions to discussions about feminism and postmodernism. In *Feminist Practice and Poststructuralist Theory,* Weedon carefully outlines the principles of poststructuralism and major areas of concern: psychoanalysis, language and subjectivity, discourse. In each area, she identifies the suitability of poststructuralist ideas for feminist use. For example, early in her discussion, Weedon uses ideas about language and discourse to analyze an image from advertising of "patriarchy at its most seductive" (15). Weedon sees in poststructuralist theory ways "to explain the working of power on behalf of specific interests and to analyze opportunities for resistance to it" (41). One example that applies to feminist music videos is her drawing on feminist psychoanalytic theory, which "develop[s] theories of women's language as a constant, repressed threat to the patriarchal symbolic order" (54–55). Female performance in some feminist music videos evokes this theoretical frame, and feminist music videos also offer "a method of decentring [sic] the hierarchical oppositions which underpin gender, race, and class oppression" (165). Weedon argues that Foucault's "work offers feminists . . . a contextualization of experience and an analysis of its constitution and ideological power" (125). Female music videos use the experience of femininity to provoke an analysis of its power.

A few years after Weedon's call for feminist practice to draw upon poststructuralist theory, Linda J. Nicholson edited a collection of essays entitled *Feminism/Postmodernism*. Postmodernists' "focus on the very criteria by which claims to knowledge are legitimized" seems promising to Nicholson (3). Like other feminist critics, Nicholson cites the breakdown of the distinction between "art and mass culture" (4), but the anthology does not pursue popular culture as a site for the exploration of feminism and postmodernism. The essays in the collection do, however, address fundamental theoretical issues about the conjunction of feminism and postmodernism. The range of approaches and of scholars, from philosophers to historians of science, is impressive, and consideration is given to a variety of applications of postmodernism and feminism.

Nicholson identifies several points of overlap between postmodernism and feminism, including the idea that both expose "the political power of the academy and knowledge claims" (5). The common interest in exposing the problems with claims to neutrality, objectivity, and reason causes Nicholson to conclude that "postmodernism would appear to be a natural ally of feminism" (5). Revealing, too, is Nicholson's inclusion of articles that express reservations about postmodernism and feminism. For example, Christine Di Stefano argues that postmodernism may be appropriate for male but not for female subjects, perhaps because women are not ready to move beyond the Enlightenment, not having experienced it as men have (65). Seyla Benhabib makes the argument—expanded in her book *Situating the Self: Gender, Community and Postmodernism in Contemporary Ethics*—that postmodernism runs the danger of being relativistic, a position that feminists cannot take because of their commitment to social change (107–30). While this collection includes some concerns about postmodernism and feminism, the very existence of an anthology entitled *Feminism/Postmodernism* moves the debate further along: if indeed there is no question that feminism and postmodernism are connected, then how will feminists use postmodernism?

While the Weedon and Nicholson books do not draw extensively on popular culture, their thorough theoretical exploration of the ways in which feminists can use postmodernist ideas justifies feminist studies of popular culture such as Angela McRobbie's *Postmodernism and Popular Culture*. McRobbie argues that "a feminist postmodernism forces us to confront questions which otherwise remain unasked and . . . in engaging with them we also find our academic practice undergoing some degree of transformation" (2). One such transformation is the consideration of popular culture forms from a new, poststructuralist perspective.

Several features of postmodernism support a feminist analysis of music videos. First, a disintegration of rigid categories encourages a new understanding of gender roles, gender being perhaps the most pervasive of all binarisms. Second, the emphasis on a breakdown between genres licenses the study of popular culture texts. Third, a new view of "reality" as fragmented and decentered encourages a shift from phallologocentrism to other texts, other approaches. Fourth, new ideas of authorship provide more space for women to act as authors—for example, as performer/authors in music videos. Feminist music videos reveal that female performers were drawing on postmodernism long before academic critics were, and the success of these artists in presenting their feminist messages to mass audiences remains a model of synthesis. Perhaps most important, feminist music videos contradict the negative views of postmodernism that result when theorists only look at texts by male authors. The portrait of postmodernism painted by feminist performers is vibrant and engaging.

A poststructuralist approach that emphasizes postmodernism allows feminists to see popular culture texts as worthy of study. In American literary criticism in the 1960s, Leslie Fiedler championed a new democratic art that would break down the distinction between "low" and "high" art; this art would resist the false elitism that characterizes modernism. Fiedler's call was reflected in high art, which began to borrow from popular culture (Andy Warhol, Roy Lichtenstein). At about the same time, Irving Howe described the same breakdown but decried generic confusion as degrading the quality of aesthetic standards. Focusing on aesthetic practices, these early discussions of postmodernism do not prepare for postmodernism as a social condition. Instead, the formalist response to changes in literary and artistic practices demonstrates the beginning of postmodernism as *both* a style and a culture. As Joseph Natoli and Linda Hutcheon explain, postmodernism is "used to describe a major (and usually a disturbing) shift away from modernity's universalizing and totalizing drive. Postmodernity's assertion of the value of inclusive 'both/and' thinking deliberately contests the exclusive 'either/or' binary opposition of modernity" (ix). Natoli and Hutcheon describe Fiedler's characterization of postmodernism, and add Susan Sontag's important valorization of the breakdown between genres.

Also important to a feminist consideration of postmodernism and music videos is Jean Baudrillard, whose emphasis on technology and fascination with American popular culture produce the ideas of the "hyperreal" and "simulacra." Baudrillard intensifies the postmodern sense that nothing is real except in its representation. "The simulacrum is never that which conceals the truth— it is the truth which conceals that there is none. The simulacrum is true" (1). By selecting American popular culture as the exemplum of the hyperreal, Baudrillard gives popular culture a status and makes it a privileged focus of postmodernism in a more emphatic way than previous theorists had done.

These developments in postmodernism justify the study of popular culture by revealing a complex picture of text in a social context. A variety of performances in addition to that of the "author" become important. For example, like Lisa Lewis (*Gender Politics and MTV: Voicing the Difference*), McRobbie asserts the importance of fans in popular culture. Cornel West writes, "For too long, the postmodern debate has remained inscribed within narrow disciplinary boundaries, insulated artistic practices, and vague formulations of men and women of letters" (90), and McRobbie draws our attention to the position of black urban music and postmodernism (discussed at length in terms of African-American women's rap in this book's final two chapters). Perhaps most important, McRobbie identifies how postmodernism breaks down a division between femininity and feminism. "The old binary opposition which put femininity at one end of the political spectrum and feminism at the other is no longer an accurate way of conceptualizing young female experience (maybe it never was). It is no longer a question of those who know (the feminist, the academics) against those who do not, or those who are the 'victims' of ideology" (158). This position is an essential one for the study of feminist music videos, for these female performers reach a far wider range of women than do feminist academics. We must throw away our own elitist notions in order to understand and appreciate the feminist postmodern music video.

While Jonathan Arac could justifiably write in 1986 that "almost no women have figured in the debate [about postmodernism]" (xi), female artists worked with postmodern forms and used such forms for a feminist message well before then. Female performers' appropriation of postmodernism deserves the attention of feminist critics. While postmodernism itself is not inherently concerned with gender, the use of postmodern art forms by female rock performers points the way toward new cultural forms for feminists. Linda Nicholson argues that "postmodern feminist theory . . . would replace unitary notions of woman and feminine subject identity with plural and complexly constructed conceptions of social identity" (35). Feminist music videos do just what Nicholson argues postmodern feminist theory could do.

A postmodern view of authorship helps a viewer understand music video "authorship." As Steven Connor writes with regard to postmodern visual arts generally, "The aesthetic that emerges from this is not quite of anonymity, but rather of simulated authorship, in which ideas of originality and repetition, authenticity and theft, are teased out to their problematic limits" (95). This emphasis on tension and on multiple participants rather than on a single author promotes resistance to the controlling interests of one ideology. The female performer in a music video, then, can be discussed as an author of the text. What Connor writes about postmodernist literary authors applies to music video performers: in their work, "the 'post' of postmodernism signifies not the fatigue of the late-comer, but the freedom and self-assertion of those who have awoken from the past" (65). Acknowledging a variety of nondirectorial influences in the music video allows the viewer to see resistance in subtle forms. By focusing on music videos as a new type of narrative, I address issues of narrative theory from a perspective that emphasizes the feminist possibilities of postmodern art forms.

This notion of multiple authorship is intimately connected with the idea that reality itself is fragmented and contradictory. Most critics, including Natoli and Hutcheon and John Docker, give Ihab Hassan credit for expanding and connecting ideas about postmodernism. Hassan connects postmodernism to "[d]econstruction's concept of a decentered world. In other words, [postmodernists] are governed by a radical epistemological and ontological doubt" (45). Postmodernism mirrors the ideas of poststructuralist critics such as Jacques Derrida, who emphasizes language and the ways in which it always already refers to the opposite of what it names, Michel Foucault, who restructures history as "archeology," and Jacques Lacan, who revises Freudian psychology to emphasize the primacy of language and the subject's relationship to language. These are all radical reenvisionings of "reality," now understood as being fragmented, arbitrary, and decentered.

How one views these shifts in attitude varies—from Howe's distaste for postmodern aesthetics to Frederic Jameson's more recent pessimism about postmodernism as a social condition. Jameson sees postmodernism as intrinsically related to late capitalism. The shallowness of postmodern culture seems to him to provide no outside place from which to resist capitalism's controlling tendencies. He sees the destruction of the unified self as producing schizophrenia (Waugh 191). In his "periodizing hypothesis," Jameson depicts postmodernism as "not merely a liberation from anxiety but a liberation from every other kind of feeling as well" (1991, 3, 52). Not surprisingly, in his pensive description of market forces controlling "the frantic economic urgency of producing fresh waves of ever more novel-seeming goods . . . at ever greater rates of turnover" (14), Jameson does not cite any female artists or producers. As I argue in *A New Species: Gender and Science in Science Fiction,* discussions of postmodernist texts that do not include feminist texts distort postmodernism by stressing only the pessimism of male artists' exhaustion. Feminist postmodern science fiction writers and feminist music video performers have quite a different, more positive engagement with postmodernism. As Patricia Waugh explains, for feminists "[t]o recognise the limitations of an ideal which was never one's own is to bear a very different relationship to its perceived loss" (194).

More recently, McRobbie uses postmodernism to justify the study of popular culture; she argues that "the superficial does not necessarily represent a decline into meaninglessness or valuelessness in culture" (4). Here she is responding to the negativity of Jameson and Baudrillard. In reviewing a Marxist perspective on postmodernism, McRobbie finds that postmodernism helpfully deflects us away from canons. She criticizes "the old Marcusian concept where a radical concept once had purchase, rapidly becomes a commodity, and in the process is washed, laundered and left out to dry" (15). Herbert Marcuse's notion of recuperation simply does not apply to a self-reflexive fluid postmodern text like a music video.

This chapter only begins the exploration of the features of postmodernism that work for female music video performers. Each chapter draws on postmodernism to explore feminist music videos, but here I will sketch out the qualities of postmodernism and provide examples that set up a foundation for the explorations in the later chapters.

Fragmentation, which has been seen as a weakness or a debility, can, in the hands of a female performer, be utilized to make powerful statements about gender stereotypes and female sex roles. By breaking up the image of femininity into pieces, a female performer can expose its construction. Music video style that relies on montage and rapid sequencing of images, and on fragments of images in each frame, calls on the viewer to break down preconceptions about "proper" roles and narratives. Fragmentation disrupts by calling into question each part of a preconception of what is "natural" and hence unquestioned.

Fragmentation is related to a breakdown between genres—in the case of music videos especially, a breakdown between high and low art. Since high art (even film, the "high art" of popular culture) has been in the control of men, female performers' insistence on the breakdown of such distinctions is a radical and disruptive act. Asserting the artificiality of a canon of art provides a place for the insertion of women and women's issues. Because video is relatively cheap and accessible, women and other disenfranchised groups can more easily make use of it than of some other forms.

Self-reflexiveness creates a sense of irony and playfulness. Related to fragmentation and the breakdown between rigid categories, self-reflexiveness is apparent in most music videos. Through images of the performers themselves, or television sets, or album covers, female performers make it clear that they are aware of the advertising function of the music video, but are self-consciously using and exposing this aspect of the form. This self-reflexivity makes it difficult to read the representations of femininity unironically and can be seen as a key to the feminism in the music videos.

Self-reflexiveness is one means by which feminist performers produce humor in their music videos. Humor is an often neglected aspect of postmodernism, perhaps because of the high seriousness and theoretical posturing of poststructuralist critics. Nevertheless, humor is a central part of postmodernism, just as breakdowns between genres and sly self-references have been staples of humor for centuries. Feminist performers have a particular need to use humor as a subversive strategy, as is shown in greater detail in chapter 2. Poststructuralist critics acknowledge parody in postmodernism, but it is a more playful humor that is at work in the efforts of feminist performers.

Sometimes the humor draws on ludicrous depictions of female sexuality. Importantly for feminism, postmodernism breaks down distinctions between social categories. Two categories thus affected are those of gender and the notion of a unified self. By depicting female sexuality in a variety of guises and historical forms, feminist music video performers use postmodernism to criticize what many feminists see as an important site of women's oppression.

This concern is so central to feminism and to feminist music videos that intertextual references, or "endless cross-referencing" or "recurring fiction" (McRobbie 18) can be seen as a common thread running through feminist music videos in a wide range of musical genres. The figures of Cinderella, Cleopatra, and the beauty pageant contestant appear repeatedly in feminist music videos. The recycling of these figures reveals a postmodernism that draws on popular culture references as source myths. These qualities of postmodernism appear in feminist music videos, but seeing the video itself as postmodern requires the use of poststructuralist sensibility to texts.

To appreciate feminist music videos, the viewer must first redefine the idea of a "text," expanding it to include a multitude of nonverbal signs and freeing it from monologic and auteurist assumptions. In a music video the performer's dress, gestures, enunciation, and look all become signs open to interpretation. Redefining "text" also means redefining "author." The author of a multi-voiced and polyphonic video is no longer, as he (or less likely she) would be, according to the auteur theory, the traditionally male director only, but is also the female performer, who interweaves and juxtaposes meanings through her delivery, her look, her gestures, and, in many cases, the music and lyrics. Well-established performers such as Janet Jackson choose their own choreographers and work with them to create an image. In this type of interpretation, the female performer is legitimated as an agent.

The star-centered institution of music videos also empowers the performer. While every video carries the name of its star and Music Television's programming emphasizes the primacy of the artist, information on music video directors is difficult to obtain; *Rock Blocks* on Music Television consists of three or more videos by a particular performer, rather than by a particular director.[1] Similarly, The Nashville Network, Country Music Television, Black Entertainment Television and VH-1 prioritize the performer's name, listing her name first, the song title second, the CD title third, and then other information afterwards. The director as well as the performer's agent undoubtedly has an equally strong hand in the final product, but poststructuralist theory allows for the discussion of the performer as an equal participant—another voice rather than a director's puppet.

The examination of three music videos from the 1980s and 1990s provides concrete and specific examples of the ways in which female performers use postmodernist techniques to create "feminist messages." Most significantly, however, these videos draw on the conventions of postmodern art forms in order to make feminist points. The form of the videos is directly related to their political content. Through fragmentation, the fusion of high and popular art, self-reflexiveness, and an emphasis on pastiche, the videos deconstruct prevailing notions of gender and sexuality.

Pat Benatar's music may not be avant-garde, but her video "Sex as a Weapon" (1985) employs the techniques of postmodernism for explicitly feminist ends. The song's popularity suggests that Music Television may be more receptive than radio to political art. The song received greater airplay on television than on radio: Eric Breitbart writes that "many [radio] stations have refused to air it because of the three-letter word in the title" (25). The self-reflexive images of dozens of video screens portray the sexual exploitation of women that Benatar condemns. At the same time that the images of women framed on television screens emphasize the self-reflexiveness of the video, the number of screens stresses fragmentation. No single image dominates the screen, and several of the images are bisected by drawings or other figures. The combination of self-reflexiveness and fragmentation stresses the power of the image and the numbing quantity of negative images of women, such as degrading advertisements, from the 1950s to the present. Like Cindy Sherman, who photographs herself in a variety of modern costumes and uses these images to expose the oppression of women, Pat Benatar uses a range of historical frames in the video images. As in other feminist videos, the rock star is foregrounded and appears as Everywoman; she plays other female characters. These appearances stress the images of women as performers, occupying artificially constructed and variable gender roles.

Other frames in the video criticize earlier gender roles, specifically those in the story of Adam and Eve, with a subtitle that describes it as "the first act of hard sell." Male roles are also criticized through a clever play on a variety of phallic images: a James Bond figure is shown loading a gun as lipsticks swivel in the lower half of the picture; the lipsticks become women as the legend "sex, violence and the worship of machismo" appears. Throughout the video, the muscle-bound male figure is depicted as ridiculous and ineffectual. He and an older man are shown staring at women, and they are rebuked by Benatar. She also rebukes the James Bond figure by taking away his gun and symbolically shooting at and destroying his machismo image. High and popular art in the video are presented in a pastiche deliberately evoked through the use of different media—photographs, video images, drawings—which form a collage effect reminiscent of other postmodern art, such as that of Barbara Kruger and Jenny Holzer, feminist artists who employ mass media to draw attention to capitalism and patriarchal power structures. Allusions to high art also appear in the images shown in the video: a large surrealistic pair of women's lips situated on a diminutive body and the words "sex as a weapon." These fragments are emphasized by the apparently roughly torn pieces of paper that frame the drawn figures of women. The series of background images depicts both male and female sex idols but primarily women, such as Marilyn Monroe, whom the culture exploited as sex objects. The series of juxtapositions of scantily clad female figures with a variety of products makes clear the specific target of Benatar's video—she is criticizing the use of women's bodies to sell products. These range from food to detergents to beer. After the first three items—women's beauty products—come household cleaner, dog food, beer and shaving cream. No brand names are given, just identifying descriptions such as "dog food" or a characteristic shape. This formlessness saves Benatar from being sued by a specific label, and, at the same time, makes the point that products are generic. Advertising makes false distinctions to increase sales. By using these images in a self-consciously critical fashion, Benatar recontextualizes them.

She employs the postmodernist techniques of fragmentation, self-reflexiveness, pastiche, and the combining of popular culture with the avant-garde. The television screens, the almost surreal combination of camera and cartoon images, and the distortion of image sizes are effects employed to criticize the exploitation of women's bodies in our culture. The images are grotesque and cartoon-like yet clearly recognizable from standard commercials. At the conclusion of the video, Benatar literally wipes the screens clear; they are obscured with snow as she jauntily crosses the picture. This is the screen left blank for the as-yet-unimaginable music video that would be freed from sexist conventions. Like other feminist performers, Benatar uses humor as a means of self-reflexiveness. She ridicules and plays with the stereotypes of men and women while explicitly preaching: "Stop using sex as a weapon." She points to psychological manipulation through the obvious phallic imagery of the lipsticks and the guns. The final image shows a model salaciously eating a hot dog; then we see an X-ray of the same activity. These frames make fun of, but also expose, the use of exploitative images in subtle sales pitches.

Her direct references to commercials and advertisements, and particularly the references to the record industry, make it clear that music videos themselves are being criticized as a part of this process. The depiction of a woman in a metallic bra is an allusion to the "Missing Persons" video in which the lead singer Dale Bozio is so attired. And the box labelled "Music Videos" and held by a scantily dressed and provocatively posed woman makes the point that music videos are just as much a part of this selling process as the other advertisements she criticizes. In a commendable piece of self-criticism, Benatar also includes the salacious cover from one of her own earlier albums, thus achieving a sort of triple self-reflexiveness. She draws, as many feminists have, from her own experience to validate her critique of the exploitation of women's bodies to sell a product. Benatar's video is one that operates as advertisement, but it does so self-consciously and, most important, politically. She manipulates the commercial and promotional aspect of the music video to criticize this aspect of the form, exposes the psychological implications of using sexual images to influence viewers, and employs the aesthetic techniques of postmodernism to critique bourgeois culture. Her combination of these three aspects makes this a stylistically ambitious and successful feminist music video, one which realizes the aesthetic potential of the form and shows that the genre can be used for social criticism even as it operates as a promotion.

The plot of "Nasty" (1986) makes it clear that Janet Jackson is criticizing sexual harassment, one of the situations to which the song's title refers. She does so by drawing upon the postmodern qualities of the breakdown between genres, self-reflexiveness, and emphasis on fragmentation, especially of subjectivity. Jackson shouts, "Stop," when she and her companions are sexually harassed by men at a movie theatre; then, in a self-reflexive move characteristic of music videos, she leaps first in front of and then into the movie screen. *Control* is the title of the album on which this song appears, and Jackson has been explicit about the importance of control to her and to the songs. As a performer, she is able to enact a control in art that is denied her in the real world. She has spoken about her own experience with sexual harassment, and how it inspired her music: "The danger hit home when a couple of guys started stalking me on the street, they were emotionally abusive, sexually threatening. Instead of running to Jimmy or Terry for protection, I took a stand. I backed them down. That's how songs like 'Nasty' and 'What Have You Done for Me Lately' were born, out of a sense of self-defense. Control meant not only taking care of myself but living in a much less protected world" (Ritz 40).

She asserts her right to privacy, to control, to be on top of a pyramid of male dancers; most significantly, she stresses her ability and power to assert her sexuality by moving between two worlds—that of the video, the movie-screen world, and that of the world outside of film, the "real" world. When she leaps out of the screen and back into the theatre, she leaves the male gaze and male desire behind; the men are trapped by their own desire in that artificial world. The men's conventional expressions of scopophilia leave them helpless in that world. Their desires literalize the notion of the "male gaze," but this is a gaze exposed by the camera angle and their positioning on the screen as one-sided and confining. They cannot leave the screen; nor can they "see" Jackson after she rejects the world of woman as sexual object. In contrast to their paralysis, Jackson can freely enter and freely leave. The setting of the movie theatre and her dexterous moving from one world to another evoke the admiration of her female backup singers, who stress the separation of the audience into lustful male gaze and approving female support. Jackson's video reveals a shift to a postmodern vision, as described by Seyla Benhabib: "*[T]he paradigm of language has replaced the paradigm of consciousness*. This shift has meant that the focus is no longer on the epistemic subject or on the private contents of its consciousness but on the public signifying activities of a collection of subjects" (208). In the video, Jackson emphasizes the activities of a group of men and women contesting public space and challenging dominance based on gender. By depicting the struggle of gender relations and by showing a woman using postmodern notions to emerge victorious over a group of male characters, Jackson points to the spaces that have opened in a postmodern art form and in a postmodern world.

The style of the video reinforces a sense of Jackson's self-assertion; as Hortense Spillers says about blues singers, Jackson expresses "the physical expression of highest self-regard and the sheer pleasure she takes in her own powers" (86). Much has been written about Jackson's physical resemblance to her famous brother, Michael, and also about the similarity in their styles of performance; yet despite obvious resemblances, an important difference remains: Janet's performances are more politically charged. In this video and in "What Have You Done for Me Lately," she directly addresses issues of sexuality from a specifically feminist point of view. Her dancing stresses her sexuality as well as her technical competency, and she responds to and rejects male advances without denying or minimizing her own body. Like Benatar, Jackson skillfully uses humor—her own wry expressions and smiles, the clever depiction of nasty men as buffoons rather than as overtly threatening or hostile figures—to defuse her potentially alienating, explicitly feminist politics. Her feminism is not compromised by this presentation but is made more appealing and engaging. The message is geared toward conversion, rather than being directed toward an already politically aware audience. Given the young target age of the music video audience, her message is appropriately cast. Her humor contrasts strikingly with the hostility and anger directed at women in so many videos by male performers. This contrast in itself exposes the misogyny of other videos.

Jackson's video contains the postmodern elements of self-reflexiveness, pastiche and an emphasis on subjectivity as performance. Like Benatar's video, Jackson's highlights the process of advertisement that defines music videos, and, again like "Sex as a Weapon," refers to the film process through the movie theatre setting. Jackson's video also draws attention to the video as performance and as promotion. The opening shots of Jackson and other patrons paying for their entry into the theatre refer to the sale being promoted through the video itself—the promotion of Jackson's album as well as of her image and political message. Although she must pay to enter the theatre, the capitalist process does not keep her from claiming the screen. This video shows that involvement in the process of capitalism and production need not equal passivity. The alienation of men and women alike that results from the sexual objectification of women is also stressed by the closing frames, which situate Jackson and her backup singers in front of the male dancers trapped on the screen. Here Jackson conveys a sense of the instability of subjectivity as she moves from viewer to performer, from acted upon to actor, and then back to the audience at the end of the video. "Nasty" also draws upon elements of pastiche as it combines contemporary backdrops with motifs of musicals from the 1940s and 1950s. The street dancing scenes summon images of contemporary dance and the musicals of mid-century. The self-reflexiveness suggests the tradition of oppressing women through film, and the pastiche similarly suggests historicity, with a vague glimpse of one of Jackson's predecessors, Aretha Franklin. As she slams the car door on her date, Jackson demands "respect," surely an allusion to Franklin's famous song. References to Aretha Franklin appear frequently in feminist music videos and connect a wide range of female performers, including Janet Jackson and Annie Lennox.

Even when she was a member of the Eurythmics, a duo consisting of Lennox and Dave Stewart, Lennox wrote a number of songs and performed in music videos that could be considered feminist. She also wrote "Sisters Are Doin' It for Themselves," a feminist song that appeared both on the Eurythmics' CD and on Aretha Franklin's CD, *Who's Zooming Who*. Her duet with Franklin in "Sisters" points again to the intertextuality and history of female rock performers. Lennox appears attired in a tuxedo and Franklin in a frilly pink dress. Lennox's extremely short hair and gender-bending attire have been a part of her performances from the beginning of her career. Her variety has been described by Barbara Pepe: "On one record, she appears to epitomize androgyny while in an ensuing video she's coyly feminine as she portrays a Frenchwoman of the baroque era, complete with powdered wig. Next thing you know, there she is, trademark scalp-chopped red locks grown out and bleached blond, leading a Motown-style blowout in a duet with the Queen of Soul herself" (12). This range of feminine styles emphasizes each as a performance, a role. Understanding her success and positioning before her solo CD and collection of music videos entitled *Diva* helps us interpret the collection.

In *Diva* (1992), Lennox has created a number of songs and videos that explore issues of gender and performance. In "The Gift," for example, she appears attired as the diva, teetering on huge platform shoes in a square in Venice. As she slowly pivots, pairs of tourists sidle up to her and have their picture taken—woman as spectacle. In "Keep Young and Beautiful," Lennox parodies a 1920s song that advises women to "keep young and beautiful if you want to be loved" and informs them that "it's your duty to be beautiful." Underscoring the historicity of the track is the scratchy sound of an old record and the period orchestra arrangement. If the other music videos don't make the irony of Lennox's singing clear, the fact that she is wearing a pair of white fluffy wings underscores the ludicrousness of the song and of social adjurations to women to "keep young and beautiful" at whatever cost. The collection of music videos repeats the themes that are introduced in the first video, "Why."

"Why" contains the postmodern aspects of the fragmented nature of subjectivity, an emphasis on the performativity of gender, the depiction of woman as spectacle, and the breakdown between high and popular culture. As the first music video in the collection, "Why" sets up these issues, which are then repeated in various motifs through the other videos. The first image we see is a

neon-lit "DIVA," which flashes off and on, erratically displaying the letter "V" and the "D," "I," and "A." This elab-
oration emphasizes "Diva" as a word that is being spelled
out—a construction, a representation. The struggle to
be or become a diva is emphasized by the ways in which
the letters apparently struggle to form, with crackling
and variation. Then, in smaller letters and in orange,
underneath "DIVA" appears Annie Lennox's name, in
what seems to be a signature. This signature emphasizes
identity and identification. As Jacques Derrida explains in
Glas, authors "sign" their names to texts both through a
proper name affixed to a title page and through the place-
ment of a name within a text. Signature theory requires
careful attention to the signing and multiple meanings
in a signature. From a Derridean perspective, Lennox's
foregrounding of the signature asks us to consider what
a name signifies. The emphasis on Lennox's signature
provides a focus on the relationship between language
and performance. Her signature and the performance
that follows call into question who or what constitutes
feminine identity.

Lennox's signature identifies her as the "author" of the
songs and music video, but her performance in the music
videos problematizes the notion of authorship in ways
that can best be understood in Foucauldian terms. What
Foucault has to say about writing in "What Is an Author?"
applies to Lennox's performance as well as to her lyrics.
In a poststructuralist frame, Lennox's performance is as
much a text as her words. In Foucault's description, "[I]t
is an interplay of signs arranged less according to its
signified content than according to very nature of the
signifier" (264). Lennox plays with the very notions of
performing and of identity by assuming the persona of

a diva for this video. The video contains her name, but her stylized and histrionic acting informs the viewer that we are not seeing the "real" Annie Lennox, whoever she might be. Again, in Foucault's words: "[T]he particular difficulties of the author's name arise—the links between the proper name and what is names are not isomorphic and do not function in the same way" (266). A music video is licensed to have an author function; that is, a music video is authored by the performer rather than by a director. But the identity of the performer is far more fluid and ambiguous than that of a director, who is assumed to have a vision and a real-life identity. Lennox's signature, then, emphasizes the fragmented nature of subjectivity, and, because of the nature of the signs in the video, especially the fragmented and destabilizing aspects of feminine constructions of identity.

The visual images underscore the construction of femininity. We first see Lennox plainly dressed and quite unadorned—she is wearing no makeup or jewelry and her hair is slicked back from her face. The camera employs a close-up, and then Lennox turns away from the camera to the mirror. This move itself foregrounds the notion of representation, as the reflection in the mirror draws our attention to the fact that we too are watching an image, a reflection, a mediation. The illusion of film is being exposed and referred to as it is in both Benatar's and Jackson's videos.

The female figure (Lennox) begins applying makeup, carefully and slowly coloring her eyebrows, curling her eyelashes, applying foundation, eye shadow. She smiles at her reflection and applies eyeliner. She grabs a scarlet feather boa and plays with it, positioning it around her shoulders and face, swinging her head back, surveying the effect. She hides her eyes behind her hands and then pulls them away, suddenly, playing "peek-a-boo" with the mirror. She appears with a dramatically towering headdress topped with feathers, long, sparkling crystal earrings, a sleeveless gold lamé dress, black fishnet stockings and platform shoes. She poses like a model, swivelling from position to position and striking dramatic poses. Lounging on a settee, she throws her head back and dons long black gloves.

The gradual and dramatic transformation of the plain feminine figure into the highly stylized and attractive diva reveals the performativity of gender. Indeed, the figure of the diva evokes images of drag queens such as Ru-Paul or the characters in the movie *Paris Is Burning* as it reminds us of the melodramatic construction of extreme femininity. The diva is clearly a performer and a performance. Lennox's video exposes the idea of woman as spectacle. Because the music video and CD were marketed as popular music, however, there is a crossover between the high art figure of the diva, traditionally an opera singer, and Lennox's own position as a member of the pop duo Eurythmics and as female pop star in her solo act.

The song's lyrics cleverly play with the visual images to emphasize the notions of fragmented subjectivity and woman as spectacle and performance. The title itself, which also serves as the refrain, asks us to question what we are viewing and hearing: "Why . . . tell me why." "Why" is an atypical music video in that Lennox does not lipsynch all the lyrics. This disjunction breaks the traditional illusion that the performer is actually singing or performing the song. Instead, her voice functions as a voiceover, stressing again the fragmented nature of subjectivity. Lennox's voice and image can be and are separated. The singer appears to be addressing a partner and singing about a troubled relationship. It's not clear, however, from the lyrics, what the sex of the partner is or what kind of relationship they're involved in. Many of the phrases work equally well if they are interpreted as being directed at the viewer/listener. Certain of the phrases are especially emphasized because Lennox lipsynchs them. "I tell myself too many times / Why don't you learn to keep your big mouth shut?" are the first lines she mouths, but their acerbity is undercut by her wry smile at the reflection of herself in the mirror. Clearly she does not intend to keep her mouth shut. In a series of lines, she positions herself and her performance: "This is the book I never read / These are the words I never said / This is the path I'll never tread / These are the dreams I'll dream instead." The series of negations ironically conveys what is unsaid or left unperformed, silences in texts. In an extreme close-up, Lennox moves toward the camera, simultaneously addressing the viewer and her absent partner. "This is how I feel? / Do you know how I feel? / I don't think you know what I feel."

Lennox's character insists on her subjectivity. She informs the viewer that we can't know her or her feelings, despite our apparent privileged insight into her dressing and posturing and emoting. Lennox's music video, then, problematizes the viewer's apparently uncomplicated relationship to the music video and the performer. Her song and video stress the performativity of music videos, especially in the construction of the female subject, who usually appears silenced. In this video, we see the process of feminine transformation and adornment, which customarily precedes the music video's normal depiction of femininity. Significantly, Lennox makes these points by drawing on the postmodern qualities of the music video form. Her music video, then, reveals how postmodernism can be used by female performers to complicate our understanding of gender and performance. By exposing the construction of femininity, she forces us to examine gender, performance and art.

These music videos provide concrete examples of how feminists can use postmodernism, showing that the theoretical parallels between postmodernism and feminism can be usefully combined to create feminist messages. Benatar's "Sex as a Weapon" reveals that, through a postmodern style, a music video can criticize sexism in advertising, including that which is found in music videos themselves. Postmodernism enables this type of criticism from within, and it is perhaps more effective than any critique made from a nonexistent, or pure, "outside." Jackson's "Nasty" employs postmodernism to expose sexual harassment and the connection between dominance and visual representation. And Lennox's "Why" uses postmodernism to describe the construction, artifice and performance associated with femininity.

These three examples suggest that postmodernism offers opportunities for feminists to use the televisual form to promote themselves but just as powerfully to criticize sexism and gender roles. These performers exemplify the ways in which feminism and postmodernism can work together. Intrinsically postmodern, music videos are a unique art form that feminist performers have successfully appropriated. Viewers can look to these feminist music videos as exemplars of how to unite theory and practice. And in the process of studying these and other feminist music videos, we can learn much about both feminism and postmodernism.

Chapter Two

"The Homecoming Queen's Got a Gun": Humor and Gender in Feminist Music Videos

Humor is the oldest form of deconstruction;
it breaks down barriers, shatters polarities, and
conducts subversive, or even liberatory, attacks
upon the reigning order.   —B. Ruby Rich

Feminist humor is, as Nancy Walker informs us in her book on the subject, "a very serious thing," especially when it appears in popular culture. Humor can be used to make trenchant criticisms of patriarchal society. Through humor, an audience can be manipulated into seeing or at least laughing at gender stereotypes or patriarchal conventions. Laughter can rupture the illusion of patriarchal authority and imperviousness. Most important, the use of humor can make a feminist message appealing to a wide audience. Feminist humor is aggressive, disturbing, disruptive. Regina Barreca explains in her introduction to *Last Laughs: Perspectives on Women and Comedy* that "women's comedy is marginal, liminal, concerned with and defined by its very exclusion from convention, by its aspects of refusal and its alliance with subversive female symbols. The difference of women is viewed as risk to culture. So it should be" (15). Humor deserves to be singled out for its liberatory power, as B. Ruby Rich argues in the epigraph to this chapter. The association of humor with postmodernism seems obvious—the very qualities of postmodernism such as self-reflexiveness, pastiche, and a breakdown between high and popular art lend themselves to humor. In addition, for an oppressed group, humor can be used as a way of bonding; Nancy Walker writes that "women have used humor to talk to each other about their human condition, to survive and frequently to protest their condition" (x). Walker's identification of the humorist as someone who is "at odds with the publicly espoused values of the culture" (9) allows her to explain the appeal of humor for American women in particular, for they are "members of a subordinate group in a culture that prides itself on equality" (x). Because humor is aggressive, "the humorist adopts at least a *stance* of superiority . . . a position of privileged insight" (25). Perhaps the most useful contribution that Walker makes is her differentiating feminist from female humor. She cites Gloria Kaufman distinguishing between feminist hopefulness and female hopelessness, a distinction that allows the viewer to appreciate the feminism of humorous music videos, which are marked by their optimism. In part because of this optimism, these feminist music videos suggest that humor can be a particularly effective tool in the arena of popular culture.

Humor is perhaps one of postmodernism's most unappreciated qualities. While most critics cite parody as a quality of postmodernism, few see the broader sense of humor that is displayed in postmodern music videos especially. Frederic Jameson proclaims, "Pastiche is blank parody, parody that has lost its sense of humor" (1988, 16). This analysis may be partly a generational blindspot, for the humor of one generation is not always that of the next. Certainly Jameson's generalization does not apply to music videos, especially feminist music videos. As this chapter will demonstrate, feminist performers use pastiche to make wry and telling commentaries about sexism and gender roles. Using humor, music videos can make critiques that are enjoyable as well as trenchant. Humor characterizes the most popular and most subversive show on MTV, *Beavis and Butt-Head*.

Humor is the defining feature of *Beavis and Butt-Head's* mass appeal. The MTV show makes fun of the music business, its consumers, and its performers. But it does so by using fragmentation, self-reflexiveness, and the breakdown between genres to point to ludicrous aspects of gender roles, capitalism, and male adolescence. Since *Beavis and Butt-Head* is discussed in great detail in chapter 4, I will turn first to humorous feminist music videos from the mid-1980s that prepare for this 1993 MTV show and then to two music videos from the 1990s that actually appeared on *Beavis and Butt-Head*.

A popular form of the music video genre, humorous music videos draw attention to the use of sex as a promotional device and to the commercial aspects of the star system of American corporate rock and roll. Video performances by artists like Pat Benatar, Julie Brown, Cyndi Lauper, Tina Turner, Annie Lennox, David Bowie, Billy Idol and Weird Al Yankovic demonstrate the ways in which performers and directors can use humor in a self-reflexive fashion to expose the commercialism of music videos and to address issues of gender formation. These videos suggest that the genre is more complex than some of its critics acknowledge. The participation of performers in self-deprecating parodies suggests that humor is a persuasive way of criticizing a popular genre from the inside. Barreca explains that "when you see humor in a situation, it implies that you can then also imagine how the situation could be altered" (19–20). While not all humorous music videos are feminist, humorous videos performed by women show that a feminist message can be conveyed in a popular genre through an inviting sense of humor. Music videos and humor both deserve to be taken seriously as strategies of resistance. Both genres have been devalued because they are part of mass culture, but, as poststructuralist theories demonstrate, popular as well as high art deserves critical attention. Feminist critics need to examine humor as a strategy because of the possibilities it offers for criticizing patriarchal institutions. Music videos present a promising case study of humor and gender.

Julie Brown's "The Homecoming Queen's Got a Gun" (1985), (The Real) Roxanne's "Roxanne's on a Roll" (1985), Tina Turner's "Typical Male" (1985), Maggie Estep's "Hey Baby" (1994), and Jill Sobule's "I Kissed a Girl" (1995) deserve particular attention as humorous feminist appropriations of the video form. Despite formal differences in their visual and musical styles, these videos promulgate a feminist message through humor. The artists use postmodern qualities—self-reflexiveness, pastiche, exaggeration and parody—to expose the ridiculousness of stereotypical gender roles and the deleterious effects such rigid stereotypes have on relationships between men and women. "The Homecoming Queen's Got a Gun" is, as its title suggests, more directly and simply humorous than many other feminist videos. The incompatibility of a sweetly attired and excessively feminine homecoming queen and the American symbol of machismo, a gun, reveals the blatant nature of Brown's attack upon sex stereotyping. Roxanne's playful irony provides an example of how performance can suggest an image of feminine strength by playing with metaphors of masculine power and authority. Turner's tongue-in-cheek title similarly suggests that gender roles will be the object of her humor, which is played out within the conventions of postmodern sensibility. Estep uses a humorous role reversal to criticize sexual harassment. These music videos use the self-reflexive humorous frame characteristic of postmodern art forms to make their feminist points. In music videos, self-reflexiveness appears in the numerous references to the filmic nature of a video, such as the television camera's filming of the homecoming queen's rampage, the appearance and servitude of a caricature of Elvis Presley in Roxanne's performance, the television set in Turner's video, a marquee trumpeting Estep's name, or the camera that appears in Sobule's video. The qualities of postmodernism used to create humor in these videos include a breakdown between the fine arts, the avant garde and the mass media; an emphasis on pastiche; and repeated self-reflexiveness. In general, postmodern art stresses paradox, contradiction and self-awareness. By calling aesthetic and cultural assumptions into question, these postmodern elements lend themselves to the deconstruction of gender through humor.

As the music video viewer watches these parodies of gender roles, she begins to realize the myriad absurdities forced on us by the construction of gender. In Julie Brown's music video, for example, the ludicrousness of the role of the homecoming (or prom) queen is illuminated by the violence of this particular young woman but also by the chagrin of the runner-up (clearly distraught at losing out) and by the panoply of pseudo-regal activities that surround the "queen." "Roxanne's on a Roll"

directs the viewer's attention to the masculine version
of the homecoming queen—the teen idol Elvis. The role
reversal between the "fan" (Roxanne) and the figure of
Elvis points to the gendered subservience and passivity
of this rock and roll pattern of male star and female fan.
Similarly, in "Typical Male," Tina Turner attacks notions
of romance, with the video pointing up the gendered
expectations and frustrations of traditional heterosexual
romance. Using an ironic role reversal, Estep attacks
the objectification of women by depicting men as objects. Sobule's far more radical "I Kissed a Girl" directly
challenges compulsory heterosexuality. As examples of
a postmodern art form, "The Homecoming Queen's
Got a Gun," "Roxanne's on a Roll," "Typical Male," "Hey
Baby" and "I Kissed a Girl" contain deconstructive and
subversive possibilities, which were emphasized by the
controversy surrounding the airing of Brown's video on
Music Television.

The response of MTV to Julie Brown's music video
attests to the power of feminist humor; the station
initially refused to air "The Homecoming Queen's Got
a Gun." After the refusal was assailed in the *New York
Times,* however, the song received brief but heavy airplay
(Kort 60), and it was later released in an anthology
of comedy music videos. Her song and video parody
conventional gender roles, allowing the viewer to see
the humor in sex-stereotyped high school role models
for young women. This depiction of high school stereotypes such as the beautiful, blond, smiling homecoming
queen, the peppy cheerleaders, the burly football player,
the geek, and the school mascot reveals how ludicrous
the heavy-handed and sexist customs of high schools
are. Like many other feminist music videos, this video

follows the detailed story lyrics closely.[1] The narrator, a narcissistic Valley Girl, describes the shooting spree of her best friend, Debi, the Homecoming Queen. The first verse tells of the narrator's elation at her friend's promenade as Homecoming Queen and includes details about her dress and the sentimental song the band is playing. The narrator breathlessly compares the scene to the Cinderella ride in Disneyland, a comparison that reveals how passive and unrealistic this cultural myth is and how it is embedded in high school ritual. The pleasant scene is punctured by someone screaming "the Homecoming Queen's got a gun" and, immediately thereafter, Debi begins shooting. Perplexed by Debi's actions, the narrator asks, "How could you do what you just did? Are you having a really bad period?" The police arrive and Debi is killed by a shot in the ear. Before she dies, however, she manages to gasp out (in response to the narrator's insistent questions), "I did it for Johnny," an enigmatic response that the narrator identifies with the movie *Citizen Kane*. Over Debi's body, the narrator meets the eyes of a handsome police officer and walks off into the crowd with him. The humor of the song is stressed by Julie Brown's playing both the role of Homecoming Queen and her Valley Girl friend.[2]

Even though "The Homecoming Queen's Got a Gun" employs a traditional narrative plot structure, Julie Brown uses a postmodern sensibility to create the humor. Playing the role of both the Homecoming Queen and her girlfriend emphasizes the artificiality of each as a role, as a representation. In this sense, Julie Brown stresses the performance qualities of femininity, just as contemporary artist Cindy Sherman does with her photographs of herself in various feminine guises. Throughout the video, humor is generated through a postmodern sensibility that relies on pastiche, self-reflexiveness and breakdown of distinctions between genres and forms. For example, the mass murder committed by the Homecoming Queen is depicted in terms of cartoon graphics. No actual or believable violence occurs, even when Debi herself dies. She leaps off her float with a perfect backward somersault, in an amusing and performative demise. Her death reminds the viewers that they are watching a representation, a film. The unrealistic and exaggerated depiction allows the viewer to laugh rather than cry as Debi kills off her schoolmates, who represent caricatures of sex stereotypes rather than believable or sympathetic characters. Secondly, humor is generated by the contrast between the narrator's attitude and the activities that she describes. Debi's friend is more concerned about her reputation and her friend's dress than she is about the carnage. Her blasé attitude is reflected in the actions of other characters—for example, the police officer who sells T-shirts as Debi continues to shoot more victims or the television reporter who seems more concerned with combing her hair than with the violence around her. The commodification of the event through the sale of T-shirts reminds viewers that they themselves are watching a promotional video. The television reporter, the camera and the microphone that Debi appropriates evoke the self-reflexiveness characteristic of postmodernism. Such incidents continually remind viewers of the artificiality of representation.

Throughout the video, which, like the song, is cowritten with Charlie Coffey, humor is produced by this basic role reversal: not only a woman, but a prim and proper homecoming queen, a cultural icon, behaves murderously. The role reversal is stressed by the huge gun that Debi totes, presumably hidden in the capacious bosom of her dress. The camp outfits—mixtures of 1960s scarves, bright colors, and mini-skirts—and the diverse mixture of fashion styles throughout the video enhance the sense of bizarre and amusing inappropriateness. Pastiche dominates, again reminding us that femininity is a construction. For example, Debi's forced beauty queen smile contrasts with her violent actions, and she puts her compact to an unconventional use when she peers into it to shoot the math teacher in a balcony behind her.

The source of the humor, then, lies in the representation of femininity. The humor in the video stems from what Walker identifies as "the myriad absurdities that women have been forced to endure in this culture" (xii)—in particular, having to act and look like Cinderella, being brainwashed into a search for romantic love, being a cheerleader, and so on. While stereotypical representations of femininity are exposed through humor, Brown also legitimates feminism. Both Brown and the viewer share a position of superiority in relation to the characters in the video. As Walker explains, "Because the humorist adopts at least the *stance* of superiority that others are accustomed to accepting on its own terms, he or she works from a position of privileged insight" (25). Watching this video, the viewer is forced into a feminist gaze. Whatever their particular ideologies, when viewers watch this video and laugh, they create a feminist community, if only temporarily and unconsciously. Nancy Walker explains that "[h]umor is a means both of establishing and testing the boundaries between groups of people . . . the community of laughter is itself an ethnicizing phenomenon as we develop a sense of we-ness laughing with others" (114). As this community is created, so is a feminist critique.

Although Brown's song is humorous, her message is serious—sexist roles breed violence and rage in women. Through the striking contrast between the prim and proper Homecoming Queen's appearance and her murderous rage, Brown exposes the hollowness of this feminine success story. Her friend the narrator is delighted with Debi's new role, but the Homecoming Queen has something besides the glory of being crowned on her mind. The narrator's description of Debi's looking like Cinderella, particularly Walt Disney's Cinderella, suggests the superficiality of this role for women. Although Debi looks like Cinderella, in Brown's feminist revision of this fairy tale, Cinderella is the aggressor rather than the victim as in the original fairy tale. "The Homecoming Queen's Got a Gun" resembles feminist fairy tales written by contemporary women authors such as Tanith Lee, Robin Morgan, and Angela Carter. Like other feminist revisions of fairy tales, Brown's parodic song serves as a warning of the suppressed anger of women trapped in traditional roles. Her Homecoming Queen functions as Sandra Gilbert and Susan Gubar suggest the Queen does in Snow White, as a symbol of how "conventional female arts *kill*" (40). Like the Queen in Snow White, Brown's Homecoming Queen is "mad," but her madness illuminates the oppressive nature of the only power available to women in a patriarchal culture.

The absence of a clear motive suggests that the role of Homecoming Queen itself produces Debi's rage. Brown stresses the pervasiveness of shallow roles for women through the Valley Girl narrator and other female voices. The anonymous narrator inadvertently reinforces the reasons for Debi's shooting spree as she describes the scene, admiring Debi's appearance without appreciating its artificiality. A chorus of female voices reiterates the importance of appearance with the lines "Stop it Debi you're making a mess / Powder burns all over your dress." The narrator struggles to find a motive for Debi's murderous rage. When Debi gasps out her last words, the narrator tries to discover who Johnny is, dismissing the one guy she knows because he was a "geek." The narrator's blindness to any other interpretation of Debi's actions is demonstrated in the final shot, when she walks off into the crowd with the cop she met over Debi's body. Her action stresses the folly of romantic love, exemplified by a romance that takes primacy over her best friend's death.

Encoded as popular culture, this video is consumed as part of a package—that is, the record packaging can be read alongside the video. Brown connects the two through parody. Her feminist message is emphasized by the album jacket that contains a mock newspaper account of the Homecoming Queen's shooting spree. The quite plausibly sensational headline on the album cover— "Sugar and Spice and Everyone's Dead"—stresses the importance of gender stereotypes in Debi's shooting spree. Significantly, Debi's first targets are the cheerleaders, who—like her—typify the secondary status of girls. On the album cover, Brown stresses the importance of sexism to Debi's outbreak. In a fake "article" about the shootings, the football coach complains, "I've always said a woman's got no place in the football field. Was I right or wasn't I?" In a decade when young women are beginning to find a place on the football field as players, the coach's comments emphasize the hostility that young women face if they challenge the construction of the feminine as passive. Debi's violent response to her sex-stereotypical role belies the purported passivity and weakness of girls.

The heart that surrounds the narrator and her new boyfriend at the video's end calls to mind the television series "Love American Style," which concluded each episode in the same fashion. This and many other allusions to representations of femininity suggest that popular culture provides its own referent system and that perhaps the best response to sexism in a genre occurs *within* that genre. For example, Brown raises the spectre of another popular depiction of apparent resistance to traditional feminine roles—the one found in Stephen King's novel *Carrie*. In contrast to King's Carrie, however, who depends on mysterious witchlike powers, Brown's murderous Homecoming Queen packs a gun. More important, Debi is a "success" in traditional terms; she does not strike out at her classmates as revenge for humiliation or ridicule. Brown's Homecoming Queen singles out representatives of the culture who are part of the structure that oppresses women—the cheerleaders, the football player, the math teacher. By eliminating them, she exposes the sexism they typify.

In "The Homecoming Queen's Got a Gun," Brown not only criticizes feminine roles, but shows how little they have changed over time. The pastiche of music and costuming emphasizes this sense of history. The music begins with the sounds of 1950s rock and roll, moves through the early 1960s, with songs like "Johnny Angel" and "The Leader of the Pack," and on to the hard rock guitar solos of the 1970s. In Brown's updated version of rock and roll rebellion, however, it is the woman, rather than a young man, who is the rebel/victim. Debi's last words about "Johnny" draw attention to those well-known songs and highlight Brown's role reversal. Ironically, Brown uses the same narrative and musical style to criticize the romantic and sexist roles promulgated by the popular songs of the early 1960s. The costumes also strengthen this parallel; Debi's dress and those of the narrator and the other actors feature elements from both the 1960s and the 1980s.

Brown suggests, however, that popular culture can also provide channels for resistance, and that 1980s retro style, which involved the appropriation of older fashions—especially, in this case, women's fashions—presents subversive possibilities. This retro style involves using postmodern pastiche to comment on gender roles; the mixture of feminine attire itself pokes fun at femininity and reveals its construction and performativity. (That the music in the 1980s allows this attack on the construction of femininity is stressed by the "article" on the album cover, in which Debi's mother confesses, "Lately [my daughter] had been listening to a lot of that new-wave type music. . . .") Like Aimee Mann, another feminist performer, Julie Brown depicts new wave music as liberating for women. Also like Mann, Brown drew on personal experience to create her feminist heroine, for she too "was a homecoming princess and rode a float similar to Debi's in the video" (Kort 60). Where Brown differs from Mann and other feminist performers is in her clever use of humor to make a didactic message appealing and engaging. Brown's music video is an example of what Barreca describes as "women us[ing] comedy to narrate their experience and so diffuse the pain" (a 22).

Brown's own career flourished after "The Homecoming Queen's Got a Gun," and she continues to press feminist claims through her use of humor. She had her own show on MTV, *Just Say Julie*, in which she functioned as a video jock, although she, unlike the other VJs, was licensed to interrupt and comment on videos as they aired. This show prefigures *Beavis and Butt-Head* in its format. As in "The Homecoming Queen's Got a Gun," Brown used humor to comment on gender roles, as, for example, she made fun of male rock stars' physiques or the size of a model's brain. Brown also starred in a film, *Earth Girls Are Easy,* based on a song from the same album as "The Homecoming Queen." The film contained a number of musical numbers staged like music videos, including the eponymous track and "Cuz I'm a Blond," a hilarious send-up of American culture's idolization and stereotyping of the dumb blonde female. Most recently, Brown starred in *Medusa: Dare to Be Truthful*, a parody of Madonna's *Truth or Dare*. In this film, which first aired on Showtime and is widely available on video, Brown uses humor to poke fun not only at the image of Madonna but also at notions of masculinity and femininity. Brown's success shows how a music video can lead to an even broader appearance of feminist message. If a music video promotes a female star with a feminist message, then its advertising function can be appropriated by a female performer.

Through its humor, Brown's ironic presentation of femininity reaches a far wider audience than a straightforward critique could. And the entertaining presentation of the song may keep the viewer's attention longer as well. For the space of a few minutes at least, the viewer is invited to laugh at a cherished icon, a representation of American femininity at its finest. It may not be Hélène Cixous's "The Laugh of the Medusa," but it is a laughter that challenges conventional notions of gendered behavior and foregrounds the artificiality of this representation of American womanhood.

While Tina Turner is not known primarily as a comedian (unlike Brown, who stars in a comedy show on the Fox Network, and who had her own comedy show with Charlie Coffey on MTV), she has made a spectacular career comeback by drawing on the same tropes used by Brown. Her tremendous popularity attests to the success of an assertive and positive feminist depiction of female humor as a commercial strategy. "Typical Male" is the second feminist video for Turner; the first was the even more popular "What's Love Got to Do with It?," a clever and straightforward assertion of female sexual desire. While that video certainly has humorous moments, it is in "Typical Male" that Turner is most explicitly and directly feminist, under the aegis of humor. While Brown focuses on gender stereotypes but only briefly alludes to their effect on male-female relationships, Turner emphasizes this aspect. Her music video relies less on lyrics and more on image to produce the humor, but the dynamic is the same as that in Brown's music video: through self-reflexiveness, pastiche, and stylized parodic violence, Turner criticizes gender stereotypes. While Brown focuses on femininity, however, Turner directs her attention to masculinity and to racism.

The patriarchy is represented in the figure of a spectacled white male. On a superficial level, the video's plot focuses on Turner's attempt to captivate this man. He represents more than a character, however, as the symbols that surround him demonstrate. The video opens with Turner pirouetting around a gigantic male shoe and leg, pantomiming her desire and inability to attract and retain the attention of a typical male. Images suggest that gender roles and sexuality are games—puzzles, toys, a chess game, and a plastic bat are all employed to evoke the idea of pleasure and competition in its most extreme and ridiculous aspects. She tries again and again to captivate this typical male, and finally, at the end of the video, she succeeds. She walks away hand-in-hand with the man, as the camera pans the giant shoe and leg, finally toppled. The end of the video answers questions the viewer might have about the point of Turner's desire to win the male character. It is a conversion rather than a scopophilic relationship, because Turner succeeds in breaking the viewer/viewed relationship when she grasps the man's hand and leads him out of the video. At the end the white male consents to be led by her; he leaves behind the symbols of patriarchy. Significantly, the edifice of a male shoe is depicted as spats, an old-fashioned and out-of-date piece of men's wear. Its demise is timely and promising. The camera angle throughout stresses the end of framing and fragmentation of woman. At no point in the video is any one part of Turner's body highlighted in the stereotypical fragmentation of a woman's body into fetishized parts. Again, this emphasis on the wholeness of Turner's effect contrasts strikingly with the attention paid in sexist music videos (like David Lee Roth's "California Girls") to female breasts, a conventional objectification of a female part. Furthermore, Turner's articulation of desire occurs in the context of a setting that continually calls patriarchal articulations into question through exaggeration and reference to toys.

Unlike Brown's, which focuses on an unenlightened narrator, Turner's video features her playing herself and exuding an air of confidence and delight, which informs us that she is not only conscious of the humor in the video but is directing it. She continually plays to the camera with a variety of smiles and knowing grins. She laughs gleefully at her performance, at her attempts to distract the man, and at the ridiculous nature of his masculine obsessions—baseball, calculations, chess. Through her laughter, she undermines and challenges the authority of patriarchy. Wrapping herself around the giant male shoe (itself a humorous rendering of patriarchy) does not indicate debasement but rather her sense of fun or challenge—with her facial expressions, she lets the viewer know from the beginning that she is determined to topple that symbol of male authority, and the viewer has no doubt of her eventual success.

Because she is the singer, and because she manipulates the camera so skillfully, Turner defies the conventional depiction of woman as object for a male gaze; it is her own gaze that determines the action of the video, her own sense of humor that she gratifies. This shift in emphasis is made clear when Turner gyrates, not directly into the camera, but to her own reflection in a series of mirrors, laughing and smiling all the while. In her video, Turner asserts the right of the woman to develop and mature through the identification of her sexual selves in the mirror. Like the videos previously mentioned, this one also explicitly evokes the idea of self-reflexiveness. Turner dances for her own pleasure as well as for that of the viewer and the male character. Her subversion of the music video form draws on her character's assumption that women feel and have a right to assert sexual desire. Again, humor is used to make this message explicit but nonthreatening. The camera plays with phallic symbols like the baseball bat, which Turner handles lightly; there can be no doubt that the violence is stylized because of the bat's ludicrous size and bright red color—it is a toy, as are the phone and the other items with which she bombards the man. Most appealing perhaps is the implicit idea of equality in a sexual relationship. The scales seen early on in the video evoke this idea, but the final image of the toppled male shoe and leg, combined with Turner's walking off hand-in-hand with the white male character, suggests a female sexuality concerned with equality rather than with replacing male dominance with female dominance. Turner does not want to erect her own shoe and leg, but asks for and implies sexual and racial parity. In this sense, casting a blond white male is particularly significant. This casting choice forces the viewer to look at the video's larger symbolic frame, which criticizes racism, and to appreciate the cooperative nature of Turner's actions. She does not attempt to reverse the power relation, but to replace it with one characterized by equality.

Significantly, she does so in a video marked by a prevailing tone of humor. The postmodern, self-reflexive nature of music videos is indicated by the frame of a television screen that Turner enters in order to grasp a plastic bat from a ballplayer. She then uses the bat in a stylized act of violence to attack the "typical male." Turner is criticizing a whole system that separates men and women—the institution and televising of sports. Here is yet another example of popular culture providing its own referent system. A music video responds to the issue of gender division created by televised sports. In another scene, Turner dances in front of a group of mirrors, reflected images that stress the film aspects of video. These images emphasize the breakdown of women into separate and alienated selves. At the same time, the mirrors stress fragmentation, for there are six of them in a row, creating a number of images, first of Turner and then of the saxophone, a phallic image that echoes the spats and, like them, represents conventional masculinity. Fragmentation also occurs in the confusing array of images presented in each frame—a plethora of graphics, actors, and large oversize props, like the gigantic red telephone receiver on which both Turner and the male actor sit. The postmodern world is dominated by exaggerated signs of everyday life, as in the work of Claes Oldenburg, who creates monumental public sculptures of objects such as buttons or clothespins. The video reminds its viewers that even everyday objects are subject to interpretation, and that these objects can become alienating, particularly if they alienate women from men. The evocation of high art and cartoon-like graphics creates a pastiche similar to the effect produced in "The Homecoming Queen's Got a Gun" but in a more overtly and stylistically humorous context.

Using a similarly playful and humorous approach (The Real) Roxanne challenges gender roles by ridiculing the masculine role of teen idol. In addition, because the idol she ridicules is Elvis, she addresses issues of race as well as gender, just as Turner does. At the same time, Roxanne uses popular culture's internal referent system, drawing on the music video form to criticize an earlier borrowing within popular culture: Elvis's appropriation of style from African-American performers. Her music video provides another example of a kind of internal critique and response within popular culture. This music video exposes Elvis's appropriation to a mass audience. Roxanne also responds to the glitz and exploitation of Las Vegas by commandeering the city for her own self-promotion, hence publicizing a female voice in a city known for its objectification of women.

(The Real) Roxanne's music video tackles the question of musical heritage and appropriation forthrightly through humor. The video opens with Roxanne stranded in the desert; then Elvis drives by in a suitably gaudy Cadillac and offers her a ride. From the moment when she thinks "Is he for real?," their roles are reversed—he becomes her chauffeur, fan and backup dancer. Elvis falls in step with her, crossing his arms and imitating her, and then later follows her dance steps on the sidewalk in Las Vegas. This humorous role reversal highlights Elvis's notorious appropriation of African-American music and places him in a subordinate position. Roxanne's refrain—"This is how it should be done"—makes the significance of the role reversal clear. The woman of color should be in control, but she exerts her role of authority with playfulness and humor. As part of her play with power, Roxanne appears in many guises—cowgirl, gambler, showgirl. As with Benatar's role-playing, the variety itself points to the various constructions of gender. Yet, as a showgirl, for example, Roxanne is not depicted in revealing full-body shots or demeaning positions. The emphasis remains on the humor of the guises rather than on the exploitation inherent in a depiction of a Las Vegas showgirl. In each mode, she clearly relishes her playacting.

Throughout the video, Roxanne asserts her right to be in control, to be at "the top of the line." She also promotes herself as a female rapper, able to move the crowd through her performance. "Watch how a real Queen moves the crowd," she declares, and she emphasizes her superiority as a rapper "sucker M. C. can't beat." She warns others to "step aside." At the end of the video, she loses at gambling, but her wry smile and her leap into the Cadillac and exit with Elvis into the sunset suggest that she's won the game she wanted to win.

In her appropriation of Elvis, Roxanne draws upon the many different and postmodern personas of this performer. The figure of the Las Vegas Elvis, rotund and wearing white-fringed leather, ridicules that of the formerly slim sex symbol and positions him and his imitators as culturally blanched—without originality. She implicitly uses this ridiculous figure and his antics to comment on Elvis's use of music from African-American culture, reclaiming it for herself as part of her identity. "Puerto Rican and proud" is how she describes herself—a stark contrast to her thought, "Is he for real?" For, of course, the many impersonators and indeed perhaps Elvis himself are not "real," but, in Baudrillard's terms, a simulacrum. Roxanne's use of a simulation of Elvis to make a feminist point about race and gender belies the pessimism of Baudrillard's vision of an America in which "[e]verything is destined to reappear as simulation" (1989, 32).

At the same time that she makes Elvis look like a buffoon, she identifies and asserts her right to a healthy, vibrant, and specifically female sexuality: "You're all dried up but I'm moist." Roxanne's many costume changes and the depictions of her gambling emphasize the construction of sexuality as a game, one she is eager and ready to play. The playfulness of the video and Roxanne's dress, look and enunciation license the interpretation of her music video as a rebuttal to more conventional and oppressive characterizations of female sexuality. The camera angle supports this reading, for the extreme close-ups of Roxanne's face resist the depiction of the female body as the object of the male gaze. "This is how it should be done," Roxanne declares, and, after watching this video, the viewer agrees. Roxanne's light tone makes clear and engaging her points about role reversal, cultural appropriation and the performativity of femininity.

Maggie Estep's "Hey Baby" is also humorous, but with a much darker, more sardonic tone. That the music video is filmed in black and white adds to the bitterness of its humor. MTV featured Estep in short ID clips, and she participated in their *Spoken Word* tour, which included music and poetry. "Hey Baby" was featured prominently on *Beavis and Butt-Head,* a tremendously popular MTV show discussed in detail in chapter 4. The appearance of Estep's music video on this show ensured it a wide audience, for *Beavis and Butt-Head* had a viewing audience of fifty million at the time Estep's video aired.

Though Estep's feminist music video aired eight years after the ones discussed earlier in this chapter, it strongly resembles the music videos of Brown, Turner and Roxanne. Like Brown, Estep exaggerates a real-life situation; while Brown lampoons the homecoming queen, Estep ridicules a male sexual harasser. As Turner creates a role reversal in which a male character is led away by a woman, Estep depicts a woman turning the tables on a man who is harassing her. And, just as Roxanne transforms Elvis into her backup dancer, Estep changes a cast of men and the harasser into mock sexual objects.

Estep not only repeats patterns, but also draws on many of the same features of postmodernism employed by Brown, Turner and Roxanne. The music video opens with a huge marquee that proclaims "MAGGIE ESTEP WHOLESALE BEEF." The sign proclaims that the video is a representation, humorously identifying its topic as being Estep's "beef" about sexual harassment. The words also draw our attention to the presentation of women as objects for consumption, like meat. Estep plays both the victim of harassment and the singer, as Brown plays dual roles in "The Homecoming Queen's Got a Gun." The video's alternation between shots of Estep confronting her harasser and of her fronting a band emphasizes the different roles that women perform. Wearing a raincoat and Doc Marten boots, Estep seems to have appropriated masculine attire. But the harasser's behavior reveals that sexual harassment is not about attire but about power and dominance.

Estep's humorous lyrics emphasize that sexual harassment is about dominance. She adopts the masculine voice to parody it. "Hey baby, yo baby, hey baby, yo baby, yo, yo, yo" are the opening words of the video. Mocking that salutation, she explains how being stalked by a harasser is frightening, but in this case she turns and confronts the man. She invites him "to go," saying "I got a huge bucket of non-dairy creamer and some time to kill," inviting him to drink with her "foul-smelling artificial milk drink" until their bladders are full, torturing themselves with the sound of a running shower. She exclaims, "I'll even spring for some of that blue stuff in the toilet. That's my idea of a good time, so how about it? You wanta?" When he asks whether she has something against men, she replies, "I don't have anything against men, just stupid men."

The images reinforce the role reversal, as the male character, who is shorter than she is, ends up on the sidewalk, with her shouting down at him. At the very end of the music video, we see Estep fingering the T-shirt of one of her band members, who are all hanging by their shirts from meathooks. They are stamped with various grades of meat, including "choice." Just in case we are not clear about the music video's message, the last frame we see is of the harasser's face, stamped "stupid."

While Estep's feminist music video is not subtle, it is quite humorous. As with Brown's portrayal of a homecoming queen, the humor stems from the role reversal. In its exaggeration of the harasser as an overdressed, sleazy man and Estep as a strong urban woman, the music video exposes harassment as a power play that will not be tolerated. The excessiveness of Estep's mock lewd response to the harasser exposes the grossness of that type of sexual overture. At the same time, having the male band members stamped with meat names again brings in the title "Wholesale Beef" and reminds viewers of pornographic movie marquees in gritty urban districts such as the one where the music video was filmed. Women are presented as pieces of meat, and Estep wants us to laugh but also to be disgusted. The title of the compact disc on which the song appears—No More Mister Nice Girl—encapsulates Estep's role reversal.

Jill Sobule's "I Kissed a Girl" has a much lighter, campier air, but her feminist message is arguably more radical, especially in the context of the extreme emphasis on heterosexuality in rock music, and, hence, in music videos. With bright lurid colors and oversized, fake-looking props, Sobule's video resembles Turner's "Typical Male." But instead of emphasizing a male-female relationship, Sobule turns to a lesbian relationship. She ridicules the trappings of conventional romance, as Brown does, but through lyrics and images provides the viewer with an alternative to compulsory heterosexuality.

The music video undoubtedly made a breakthrough on MTV in terms of its explicit reference to lesbian sex because of its light humorous tone. Whereas Estep's music is rap, Sobule's is a light upbeat pop tune. Like Turner, Sobule uses close-ups and facial gestures to convey surprise, wry pleasure and an air of fun and delight. As she narrates the experience of kissing a girl "for the first time," we see parodied scenes of a suburban neighborhood. The very first scene shows an all-American, blond newspaper boy, with several tiny American flags on his bike, throwing newspapers onto the lawns of absurdly colored cardboard houses. These bizarre houses and the white picket fences askew in front of them constitute a pastiche that ridicules the vision of surburban conformity and traditional family. Their artificiality is obvious even to Beavis and Butt-Head, two characters who watch the video carefully. Beavis complains, "Those houses look fake," and Butt-Head responds, "Of course they do—that's the whole point of college music—to make the suburbs look bad."

Two housewives emerge from their houses to get their newspapers. Sporting fifties retro hairstyles that evoke the beehives of the rock group the B-52s, one woman wears an apron, the other pearls. They direct fake, forced smiles at each other and wave. Peering from their windows, each watches as the other trims a hedge or waters her flowers. We see them looking at each other. One wears a scarf, the other carries Tupperware—accoutrements that signal 1950s suburban housewives. But then the two women are alone, sitting at opposite ends of a sofa. A huge fish mounted over the fireplace looms, a giant soon-to-be subverted symbol of patriarchy. Like Brown, Sobule adds to the sense and critique of the construction of femininity by playing herself—the artist singing the song—and also one of the two women. At the end of this sequence, the women sit close together on the sofa, and one woman places her hand on the other's thigh. In the words of the song, "We laughed at the world . . . We had a drink, we had a smoke, she took off her overcoat . . . I kissed a girl."

But the song does more than simply champion the pleasures of kissing a girl. In a sequence after the one in which the women are on the sofa, we see their husbands come home from work, hard hats on, lunch pails in hand.

The husband of Sobule's character turns out to be the heartthrob model Fabio. He takes off his hat and shakes his long beautiful hair, a gender-bending surprise. Then we see Fabio and Sobule in a variety of traditional heterosexual poses—Fabio as himself, Sobule as a mermaid in his arms; Sobule as a medieval lady, Fabio as a knight in armor. Subsequently we see the other woman imagining Sobule as a mermaid and herself as her lover, wearing a face mask and diving suit. They both look happy and smile at the camera. Since Fabio achieved fame as a cover model for romances, his casting here again shows a critique of one popular culture form within another, romances being exposed in a music video.

The music video also shows the two women at a cookout, talking to their husbands but playing footsie with each other under the table. The music video concludes with the two women exiting their front doors again, each apparently nine months pregnant. They look at each other, sigh and turn back into their homes, apparently trapped. Rather than reifying compulsory heterosexuality, this music video makes fun of suburbia, as Butt-Head notes, but also more specifically of heterosexuality. The women's delight in each other and the campy setting make it clear that a lesbian relationship can be a pleasure.

At the very end of the music video, Sobule herself falls back, smiling, onto a bed, with the fake houses in the background. The refrain "I kissed a girl" emphasizes action and passion and fun. It is difficult to listen to a traditional heterosexual love song after hearing Sobule's recasting of kissing and seeing her entertaining music video, because "I Kissed a Girl" compellingly reframes romance. As Brown reinvents and alters the homecoming queen, Sobule reinvents the first kiss.

Since, as many critics have argued, humor is socially constructed, feminist critics must more carefully examine the site of its construction and be ready to look for humor in unexpected places. Music videos display the sense of doubleness, of play and diversity. Humor, as these examples suggest, can be a powerful and persuasive means of promoting a feminist message. Through humor, music videos also offer moments of resistance to abusive stereotyping of women. Exposing sexism through ridicule is an entertaining and compelling way to rebut the misogyny of many music videos. As Julie Brown says, "[I]f we can laugh at the idea of women as only sexual objects, it's good . . . anytime you make people laugh, it puts a distance between them and what they're laughing at. And then they can get a better look at it" (Kort 61). These humorous music videos show that the "image" of woman is a more complex one than the picture of woman as sex object so familiar to us, and that humor is a strategy that can and should be embraced by feminists, both as a means of resistance within a genre and also as a means of reaching a wide audience. That these female performers draw on postmodernism to create the humor shows that the two strategies are closely related.

Chapter Three

"Justify My Love": Music Videos and the Construction of Sexuality

Nothing is less certain today than sex, behind the liberation of its discourse. And nothing today is less certain than desire, behind the proliferation of its images.   —Baudrillard, *Seduction*

Since MTV first began broadcasting in 1981, music videos have been castigated for their explicit portrayal of sexuality. Many critics, feminist and otherwise, have damned MTV's depiction of women, as though music videos were unique in their exploitation of female bodies.[1] In the context of this book's evaluation of music videos, however, I ask the reader to reconsider the standard, reductive dismissal of music video depictions of sexuality, especially female sexuality. On MTV, as elsewhere, sexuality is a construction, and there is a variety of portrayals of sexuality. To make their case, critics of music videos assume that there is but one depiction of sexuality and that any representation will be exploitative. However, as the theoretical discussions in chapters 1 and 2 suggest, especially from a poststructuralist perspective, popular culture texts are complex and multilayered. While there certainly are many disgusting and deplorable representations of women's bodies in music videos, many others problematize the whole notion of sexuality.[2] As John Leland notes, all-female groups like Salt 'n Pepa and

En Vogue "play sex as sex, but also as politics. At a time when popular music is particularly hostile to women, theirs is a celebration of female sexual control" (56). It may be this complicated approach to sexuality that explains the attacks on music videos from both the left and the right—the left looking for a unified, essentialist sexuality that privileges and protects the feminine, while critics on the right oppose the representation of sexuality at all. In contrast, this chapter explores the issue of sexuality as a heterogeneous postmodern construct in music videos.

Since many feminists and critics do not watch music videos on a regular or systematic basis, they may be unaware of how slanted and distorted are the attacks on music video depictions of sexuality. Attacks on music videos often take the same form as those on other arts that challenge dominant forms of sexuality, such as Robert Mapplethorpe's photographs. The Reverend Donald Wildmon, for example, through his American Family Association, is notorious for excerpting pieces of an artwork that are offensive and using the fragments to justify censorship or the withholding of National Endowment for the Arts grants from particular artists. Similar distortions appear in documentaries attacking the depiction of sexuality in music videos. A thirty-eight-minute video entitled *Rising to the Challenge: A Revealing Look at the Pied Pipers of Today's Rock 'n' Roll*, produced by the Parents' Music Resource Center (Tipper Gore and company) in 1991, contains only excerpts from music videos. As the title of its documentary suggests, the Parents' Music Resource Center (PMRC) is interested primarily in showing that music videos are violent and damaging to children. To make this point, the documentary relies on excerpts from some music videos to make the argument that the genre itself is dangerous. Similarly, a recent "exposé" of MTV made by Sut Jhally, a professor of communications at the University of Massachusetts, *Dreamworlds*, runs fifty-five minutes, includes images from more than 150 music videos, and strips the music from the images. To make their case, both documentaries must isolate images and distort the normal viewing practice, in which a variety of complete music videos appear. Such a proceeding is a cheap, easy and sloppy way to condemn the depiction of sexuality in music videos. These recastings of music videos create a false unity of image, implying a seamless construction of sexuality.

The implicit elitism of both the conservative (PMRC) and the Marxist (Jhally) assumes that music video viewers and performers can only be the dupes of media images, rather than being informed consumers and fans in the active sense of fandom that Lisa A. Lewis describes in some detail in *Gender Politics and MTV* and *The Adoring Audience: Fan Culture and Popular Media*. The false totalizing pessimism of both conservative and Marxist positions assumes that there is only one interpretation of images of sexuality and that it is negative. Even so perceptive a critic of music videos as Andrew Goodwin falls into the trap, which he criticizes throughout his book, of oversimplifying—in this case concerning the depiction of women in music videos. Relying primarily on Jhally, who commits the error Goodwin identifies of separating image and music, Goodwin damns "the routine denial of subjectivity to women in music videos and their repeated display as helpers, assistants, objects of lust, groupies, backup singers, and so on" (186). He even claims "the common comparison between MTV and

porn is in fact insulting to pornographers" (186). Not un-
related is Goodwin's similarly curt dismissal of postmodernism and music videos. He claims that "music video
in general and MTV in particular both represent poor
choices of case studies for advocates of postmodern
theory" (17). Ignoring feminist music videos, Goodwin
makes the familiar claim that postmodernism is apolitical
(176). As the music videos discussed in this book reveal,
however, feminism and postmodernism work together in
some music videos. Feminism and postmodernism can
even help feminists deal with sexuality, a topic fraught
with conflict for feminists. Feminist music videos that
deal with sexuality support Baudrillard's postmodern
description of the power of seduction as "a power of
attraction and distraction, of absorption and fascination,
a power that cause[s] the collapse of not just sex, but
the real in general—a power of defiance" (1990, 81).
Used by female performers, then, an emphasis on the
construction and performativity of sexuality challenges
gender categories and roles.

   In part the centrality of music videos in this debate has
been produced by conservative groups like Parents' Music Resource Center and Marxists like Sut Jhally. While
these critics of music videos are not completely wrong,
neither are they exactly right. What this chapter does is
to correct their excesses by examining music videos that
resist the dominant exploitative depiction of women.
Such music videos should be considered carefully, for airing as they do in juxtaposition with other videos, feminist
music videos provide a far more challenging resistance
to sexist depiction of women than do documentaries
produced by conservative groups or university profes-
sors determined to damn the genre. Most important,

female performers draw on the postmodern decentering qualities of the genre and our culture to criticize old-fashioned patriarchal ideas about female sexuality.

What is needed is an assessment of the depiction of sexuality in music videos that considers the range of images appearing in the genre and the underlying issues of construction and performativity. This chapter provides a much-needed corrective to the slanted attacks against sexuality in music videos. The music videos discussed in this chapter demonstrate that the depiction of sexuality in music videos can be complex and, from my perspective, even empowering for women. What Parents' Music Resource Center and Sut Jhally do is a version of a critique of sexuality that can be traced back to nineteenth-century debates about the role of woman as either angel or whore.

This chapter's analysis of music videos examines the place of sexuality in feminism. The music video performers discussed here confront the problem of "how to be overtly sexual and still be a feminist" (Leland 57). Historically, sexuality has been seen as a danger to women, something that needed to be carefully controlled and circumscribed by women themselves. Sexuality was seen as a source of danger by many nineteenth-century feminists (see Gordon and DuBois), and this pattern continues into the twentieth century in the antipornography movement in feminism (Willis 1983). As Jacqueline Rose explains, in "the debate about sexuality . . . the cinematic image is taken as both the model of and term for a process of representation through which sexual difference is constructed and maintained" (199). Rose's acknowledgment of the postmodern frame for sexuality is crucial for music videos. The analysis of music videos is one arena in which we can explore a conflict between two different feminist points of view. The "pro-sex" or anticensorship (Williams) perspective is represented by feminists like Ellen Willis and the feminists who edited a collection of pornography entitled *Caught Looking*. These feminists see an open expression and acceptance of all types of sexuality as central to the liberation of women. The other view is held by those like Andrea Dworkin and Catherine MacKinnon who describe themselves as opposed to degrading pornographic depictions of women.[3] Dworkin and MacKinnon might consider music videos pornographic, but anticensorship feminists can find much to justify their position in music video exposés of the construction of sexuality. Such a perspective requires the viewer to adopt a position on sexuality such as that enunciated by Carole S. Vance. In the introduction to *Pleasure and Danger: Exploring Female Sexuality*, she writes that "to assume that symbols have a unitary meaning, the one dominant culture assigns them, is to fail to investigate" (15). She continues, explaining that feminism "must understand pleasure as life-affirming, empowering" and "insist that women are sexual subjects, sexual actors, sexual agents" (24). Her anthology contains numerous articles from the controversial Barnard conference on sexuality that serve to support her claims. This chapter will also demonstrate that women can act as sexual actors and agents in music videos. Indeed, music videos provide a site for the exploration of the ways in which female performers can deconstruct the dominant discourses of sexuality.

While some music videos attack the representation of sexuality by problematizing it, some feminist music videos deal with sexuality in a forthright, nonjudgmental, and entertaining fashion. By depicting sexuality as something that women have a right to express and control, these music videos contradict the stereotypical and limited depiction of women's bodies in other music videos. In some videos, as Goodwin acknowledges, dancing itself becomes a way of communicating sexuality and sexual desire: "Dance as an assertive act linked to protofeminist lyrics may also work as 'access signs' or 'discovery signs' (to use Lisa Lewis's terms . . .) providing for female appropriation of male movements (Joan Jett, I LOVE ROCK 'N' ROLL) or a validation of female dancing (Madonna, INTO THE GROOVE, Pat Benatar, LOVE IS A BATTLEFIELD)" (69–70).

Dancing and sexuality can be used by female performers to assert feminist messages. For example, in Pat Benatar's "Sex as a Weapon," a lively and clever music video, she not only exposes the use of sex to sell products but also acknowledges her own previous involvement in this system. In a related vein, Salt 'n Pepa, a feminist rap group, appear in "Let's Talk About Sex" (1992), a music video that directly asserts both the right of women to express sexual desire and the right to decide when, where and how to have sex. Salt 'n Pepa make it clear that they believe that women have the right to say no and yes as they decide. Similarly, in M. C. Lyte's rap dialogue with Positive K, Lyte asserts her right to be sexual, but also to quote from her video, "I'm Not Having It" (1985), to the pursuing male.

In the more recent "Shoop" (1993), Salt 'n Pepa make an explicit role reversal in which they gaze at men's bodies and evaluate them. In a playful postmodern spirit of invention, "shoop" refers to sex, but Salt 'n Pepa coin a new word because the sex they describe is female-centered. With a frank appreciation of the male body, Salt 'n Pepa sample romantic songs from the past, but reconfigure them in a female voice. Replacing male singers emoting as they sing "You taught me what to do" or "Don't know how you do the voodoo that you do," Salt 'n Pepa take turns parodying romantic music. Their postmodern pastiche also evokes a girlie show, as the group performs on stage with a neon "GIRLS, GIRLS, GIRLS" and a neon "X." But Salt 'n Pepa dance with men and other women on this stage, and they turn to gaze directly at the camera, making clear their awareness of sex as performance.

The stage scenes are cut with scenes of the women expressing sexual desire in everyday locales: a boardwalk, a basketball court, on the beach. Men are depicted and sung about as objects of female sexual desire, but the role reversal is not a complete turnaround; the music video depicts the men as active, and they are given a voice, in stark contrast to the standard portrayal of women as passive and voiceless in music videos such as David Lee Roth's "California Girls" or Robert Palmer's "Addicted to Love." "Shoop" is an explicit and engaging portrait of women acknowledging and naming their heterosexual desire.

As we saw in the last chapter, Jill Sobule's "I Kissed a Girl" (1995) wryly tells the story of kissing a girl for the first time. This music video is a rare but significant representation of lesbian sexuality. "I Kissed a Girl" may be a sign of change in the world of music videos. Broadcast television, in shows like "L.A. Law," "Roseanne," and "Picket Fences," has already featured lesbian characters and kisses. But while those shows deal with the lesbian character as a problem, this music video relishes the pleasure of the lesbian kiss. With a mock suburban setting—brightly colored cardboard house backdrops—the music video shows two female neighbors shyly discovering their attraction for each other. Like "Shoop," the music video plays with conventions of heterosexual romance, as the husband of one of the characters is played by Fabio, the male model featured on the covers of romance novels and on his own calendar. The video's use of fragmentation, pastiche, and self-reflexivity and its emphasis on the representations of sexuality make it a wry postmodern text.

In "Nasty" Janet Jackson also insists on the right of women to feel sexual desire, one meaning of the word "nasty," but she frames her sexual desire in terms of her right to control (*Control* is the title of the CD on which this track appears). In her new videos, Jackson explains that the theme of sexuality and a woman's control over sexuality continues. She describes the CD as being about "[a] woman who finally feels good enough about her sexuality to demand a man's respect. It's insulting to be seen as some object; he must call her by name. It's not a brazen demand—I didn't want to be obnoxious—but I wanted to be clear. Women want satisfaction. And so did men. But to get it, you must ask for it. Know what you need. Say what you want" (Ritz 41).

Jackson's attitude can be traced back to its historical roots in blues singers. In an article on black female sexuality, Hortense Spillers discusses blues singers and sexuality in terms that apply equally well to contemporary music video performers. "The singer is likely closer to the poetry of black female experience than we might think, not so much, interestingly enough, in the words of her music, but in the sense of dramatic confrontation between ego and the world that the vocalist herself embodies" (Spillers 86). This sense of duality, of confrontation, is central to the female appropriation of the music video form, and it helps to explain why so many African-American female performers are in the forefront of this subversion. African-American female performers draw upon a tradition in which, as Spillers notes, the singer's "sexuality is precisely the physical expression of the highest self-regard and often the sheer pleasure she takes in her own powers" (88). Other feminists have explained more generally that it is rock and roll that liberates female sexuality: "[R]ock music . . . provided me and a lot of women with a channel for saying 'I want,' for asserting our sexuality without apologies and without having to pretty up every passion with the traditionally 'feminine' desire for true love and marriage and that was a useful step toward liberation" (Echols 227).

Looking closely at these videos' depictions of sexuality enables us to see that the portrayals are not exclusively oppressive, and that female performers are able to use their sexuality to promote images of women who have strong sexual desires and are not reduced to sexual objects. These performers draw upon what Audre Lorde describes in her essay "The Erotic as Power." Lorde criticizes "the false belief that only by a suppression of the erotic within our lives and consciousness can women be truly strong" (53). She describes the erotic as "an assertion of the lifeforce of women; of that creative energy empowered, the knowledge and use of which we are now reclaiming in our language, our history, our dancing, our loving, our work, our lives" (55). This reclamation and role reversal does, however, leave unchallenged the fundamental premise of sexuality as a simple, straightforward, natural instinct.

By revealing that sexuality is a construction and a performance (a postmodern view), other music video performers can direct the viewer's attention to the artificiality of gender roles. To understand how these female performers manipulate film conventions and traditions, we must first consider Laura Mulvey's ground-breaking and influential analysis. Mulvey began and defines the discussion of what she identifies as "the male gaze" in an article entitled "Visual Pleasure and Narrative Cinema." She describes how "unchallenged, mainstream film coded the erotic into the language of the dominant patriarchal order" (16). In her analysis, film inherently positions "woman displayed as the *leitmotif* of erotic spectacle" (19). "WOMAN AS IMAGE, MAN AS BEARER OF THE LOOK" has shaped much subsequent discussion of feminism and film. Feminist music video performers expose this tradition by reversing it, by appropriating the gaze for themselves, or by exposing the false unity of the male gaze as the only possible viewing position. Music videos use the male gaze and comment upon it in a variety of ways. The exposure and exploitation of the male gaze by many female and some male performers is more complicated and sophisticated than the overt appropriation of the male gaze for women, but both approaches challenge the dominant depiction of woman in film.

There are a number of ways in which music videos point to the construction and artifice involved in the representation of sexuality. The group En Vogue uses and exposes the male gaze in ways that emphasize the performance of sexuality. Madonna's infamous music video "Justify My Love" belongs in this discussion, for no other single music video performer has generated quite so much controversy about sexuality.

We should consider the ways in which female performers can manipulate their position as objects for a male gaze and, at the same time, comment upon "the male gaze." En Vogue, a popular all-female singing group, has gained much attention for their music videos, especially during the 1993 MTV Music Video Awards show, where they swept the awards. En Vogue's music videos are also available on their own documentary, *Funky Divas* (available at your local video store), which contains three of the music videos from the *Funky Divas* CD, as well as interviews with all four members of the group. In the video, the group discusses the significance of their use of the word "diva," which evokes Annie Lennox's appropriation of the term about the same time. En Vogue decided to use the title "Funky Divas" after "we looked up the word diva and it meant female lead vocalist in the theater." The women stress that they are all divas; each has a chance in the spotlight, and they are aware of and comfortable with the association of performance and staging that the word "diva" implies. Similarly, Terry Ellis explains that the group's goals involve more than fashion. "En Vogue means more than just in step with fashion. . . . It means being an African-American woman who projects a positive image" (*Ebony* 98). Their music videos are one way in which the group projects a positive image. In the documentary video, they are shown practicing for the music video production, and then we finally see the music videos themselves, which are interspersed between segments of the interviews.

The music video documentary *Funky Divas* and the group's acceptance speech during the MTV music videos awards both serve to underscore what is a theme of all their music videos: the construction and performativity of female sexuality. While En Vogue's music videos all contain seductive moves and salacious costuming, in the interviews that break up the music videos, we see them clad in unglamorous practice attire: oversize T-shirt, shirt and loose skirt, plain leotards. Three members of the group have their hair back in tight buns; the hair of the fourth member is cut short. This image presents a startling contrast to the elaborate costumes and wigs that they wear in their music videos. Similarly, when they speak directly to the camera, as they do throughout most of the video, we see close-ups of their faces and their own hair rather than the dramatic wigs that they wear during the music videos. Their faces are hardly made up at all, and they wear a range of different clothes and accessories: Terry Ellis has on an African hat and coin earrings, Cindy Herron a shiny blue sweat outfit, Dawn Robinson a loose white blouse, and Maxine Jones a denim shirt, and her short hair sticks straight up. The juxtaposition with their appearances in the music videos is dramatic and shocking, their "natural" selves contrasting with those other extreme and revealing styles. In a similar vein, as my Colby College student Sally Reis pointed out, when they were telecast from Milwaukee (where they were touring) during the MTV Music Video Awards show, they appeared again in plain attire, not made up, backstage. In itself, these contrasts are not particularly shocking; what is fascinating is how they underscore a theme already present in the music videos themselves: the performativity, construction and artificiality of feminine sexuality.

In their performances, the members of En Vogue skirt a fine line between exploitation of their bodies and an assertion of their right to have, display, and enjoy their bodies. Like Madonna, En Vogue appears to enjoy playing with the tensions surrounding female sexuality and the female body. Their first music video from *Funky Divas* is "You're Never Gonna Get It." As the title suggests, the singers taunt not only the male character who is Maxine's ex-boyfriend, but also the male viewer, represented by a male dancer who is sheathed in plastic that obscures his features, suggesting his symbolic function as a stand-in for all men. The lyrics laud women controlling their own sexuality and rebuke the misbehaving lover, who is informed that "you had your chance to make a change." The rebuke is depicted physically as well as verbally: in one brief scene, a woman, attired in a formfitting dress and high heels, meets a man in an apartment, slaps him in the face, and then nudges him with her shoe before walking over his supine body. Interspersed in this scene are shots of the male dancer reacting as the woman strikes the man, again suggesting that the male represents all men. We don't see the male actor's features, just the back of his head and his crumpled form. What is being denied him is clearly the singer's sexuality: "My loving—you're never gonna get it," sings Maxine. Dawn provides backup support, singing, "What makes you think you can just walk back into her life?" Then all four women together harmonize, "Never gonna get it." The lyrics make it perfectly clear where the lover failed: "Maybe next time you'll give your woman a little respect." With this line, En Vogue echoes a theme present in the work of many feminist performers, from Aretha Franklin to Janet Jackson and Annie Lennox.

The images in the music video play with the lyrics, but also assert the sexual desirability of all four singers. The way that the women stride and posture together also underscores their support for each other and their unanimity about their right to control their sexuality. Clad in identical silver sheaths, they glide out seductively, emphasizing their sexual attractiveness and what is lost by failing to give your woman respect. Their dancing exemplifies the possibility of "dance as an assertive act" (Goodwin 69). Similarly, they appear in black tights and identical curly wigs. In one shot, Terry affirms Maxine's pronouncements—"hmm-hmm—that's right," she declares. Their seductive images provide them with a source of power over men and control of their own sexuality. This idea of women having power because of their sexual allure is not overtly feminist, but it does provide an antidote to the voicelessness and anonymity of so many other female bodies in the backgrounds of music videos produced and performed by men. The strength and power of women controlling their own sexuality is emphasized by Maxine's performance. Several times, she throws her head back defiantly as she declares, "You're never gonna get it." Her intonation deepens as she emphatically repeats "not this time." The performance makes the message of feminine strength clear and unequivocal. At the same time, Maxine's assertion of the right to control her own sexuality and the support she receives from the other members of the group constitute a depiction of women working together to make the erotic their own.

In between this video and the next are scenes that deconstruct "You're Never Gonna Get It." We are shown the music video being filmed from different angles, the blue backdrop that is filled in with special effects in the final version, and the group practicing their moves. Then we see earlier scenes of En Vogue practicing in a studio. Here they appear in unglamorous plain attire. They are shown being coached by a man in synchronizing their lips to the music; then we see the slate being slammed shut, signifying the beginning of a filming sequence. These scenes make the performativity of music videos and femininity clear. The emphasis on performance is elaborated in the first frames of "Giving Him Something He Can Feel." In shots strongly reminiscent of those in Annie Lennox's "Why," the viewer sees makeup—eyebrow color, eyeliner and lipstick—being applied. The extreme close-up emphasizes the construction of feminine sexuality, which is the theme of "Giving Him Something He Can Feel."

This music video makes clear the contrast between female empowerment and male powerlessness by including not just one male character, as in "You're Never Gonna Get It," but dozens of them in an audience. In "Giving Him Something He Can Feel," even the title is ironic. En Vogue is depicted as actually performing at a club—perhaps a version of the new "gentleman's clubs" that feature strippers, for there is not a single female in the audience. The performance, however, is not about feeling but about seeing. En Vogue appears on a raised stage and a red velvet curtain goes up. The pull-back camera shots reveal that there is considerable distance between the group and the men. As they perform, they demonstrate the creation and the construction of sexual desire.

Clad in skin-tight red dresses with cups in the tops and long black gloves, the performers sing sultrily and dance seductively. The audience of well-dressed African-American men responds instantly and electrically to the performance. They are obviously both overcome and discombobulated by En Vogue. The men's heads follow the performers' every move, and the various male characters quaff champagne, loosen a tie, wipe sweat from a brow. In a clear reversal of the traditional expectations, it is a male character who evokes the suggestion of a striptease, loosening his tie and finally removing it and tossing it aside. Members of the audience wring their hands, nervously wipe sweat from their upper lips, repeatedly fan themselves with their hats. One man removes his wedding ring and places it in his suit pocket. The men are sitting at least ten feet from the stage, a distance that is revealed through several shots from the back of the room and from behind the stage. They all lean forward, following the singers' moves. The extreme nature of the audience's reaction, the fact that the audience is entirely male, and the computer enhancement of En Vogue's bodies make it clear that the video is exposing the performativity of feminine sexuality in a male-dominated society.

The music video "Free Your Mind" makes this exposé of the construction of sexuality explicit. The first shots show a camera sliding over the models' runway. Rows of fashion photographers repeatedly take pictures, emphasizing the power of the image. A similar move shows the women wearing wigs. As one sings "Don't blame me if I have straight hair," she pulls on a braid that is obviously false. The women parade down the runway wearing highly stylized and bizarre outfits, giving another version of their performance of femininity.

The lyrics reinforce this reading of the text, being explicit about the male gaze: "I can't look without being watched." The right of women to assert their bodies is claimed in the first lines of the song: "I wear tight clothing and high-heeled shoes; it doesn't mean that I'm a prostitute." As they stride down what they themselves describe as a futuristic fashion show platform, En Vogue again makes it obvious they are performing female sexuality. They assert their right to date men of any color. In an explicit address about both race and sexuality, they declare, "Before you can read me, you got to learn how to see me." They dance with each other and wave their cloaks, dramatically emphasizing the lyrics. Their reclamation of the fashion show platform and the endowing of models with voices are ways of appropriating fashion and allowing women to express their opinions about race and gender and sexuality. As Terry says, "You see us looking different ways because we like to free our minds and just do different things. To us it's an attitude." "Attitude" in music video terms requires that we take seriously En Vogue and their emphasis on performing sexuality.

More than any other music video performer, Madonna has revealed the construction and performativity of sexuality. In her many commentaries about sexuality, there are similar messages about control and about controlling and exposing the male gaze. But because Madonna is a solo performer, the solidarity and strength provided by a group of four women is missing from her work. The message of solidarity is, however, conveyed in Madonna's representations of many femininities through her self. Her work presents a more radical challenge to patriarchal definitions of sexuality because she positions not only female sexuality as a construct but also male sexualities. Ellen Willis praises "Madonna's bravura performance," in which she uses "the pervasive eroticism of [American] mass media . . . to attack . . . its virulent anti-sexual moralism" (xxxv). She describes Madonna's approach as "turning all the stock pop-sex images of women into weapons of the self-willed, protean, sexual female, exaggerating femininity till it suggests impersonation, insisting that sex is an artifact, a wholly constructed fantasy, but no less primal for that" (1992b, xxxv). Willis's description of Madonna emphasizes her postmodernist approach to femininity and its focus on the construction of gender and sexuality. Unlike any other mainstream performer, she moves from heterosexuality, absolutely unquestioned in most music videos, to other forms of sexuality.

Like Julie Brown's "The Homecoming Queen's Got a Gun," which provoked a great deal of controversy and media attention, Madonna's performances must be taken seriously because they attract so much attention. She forces us to examine and rethink conventional pieties about gender roles and sexuality. Madonna has already been the subject of numerous articles and books, including Mark Bego's *Madonna: Blonde Ambition* and Susan McClary's *Feminine Endings: Music, Gender and Sexuality*, but she belongs in this discussion of sexuality and music videos because no performer has dealt more explicitly with sexuality. The music videos "Express Yourself" and "Open Your Heart" depict Madonna in the role of sexual subject but one who escapes the confines of the role. Madonna's most daring and controversial music video, though, is "Justify My Love," which was banned from MTV and then sold in an almost unprecedented fashion, as a single music video at a cost of $9.95.[4] "Justify My Love" demands consideration, because, in this video, Madonna depicts a wide range of possibilities for sexuality, a number of rooms in that hotel. The hotel stands for illicit sexuality, outside the domestic sphere, as a totally commercial space, and it functions as a gateway, a stop on the journey of sexuality. As Richard Goldstein describes it, in "Justify My Love," Madonna evokes "the breakdown of sexual categories." Goldstein also praises the music video's "dissident attitude toward gender and sexuality" (52).

We first see Madonna carrying a suitcase, with her hand to her brow, looking tired and exhausted. Then, through an open door, she sees staring out at her a woman with cropped short hair, wearing long pearls, black strips of cloth, and black gloves. The next shot reveals a man turning on a bed. Madonna then declares, "I want." When she crouches down, viewers see a set of stockings and garters, and then the camera flashes to other scenes of sexuality: a man posing and gyrating, a man watching Madonna being kissed by an androgynous figure, a couple watching themselves in a mirror. Madonna's first partner appears attired in a leather harness, and one androgynous character draws a moustache on another similarly ambiguous person. Throughout, in a soft husky voice, Madonna makes demands: "Talk to me," "Love me—that's right." She exits, with her hair tousled and her hand only partially covering her gleeful smile; then she laughs. The music video ends with these words on a black screen: "Poor is the man whose pleasures depend upon the permission of another."

The music video's many plays on the indeterminancy of gender stress the construction and performativity of sexuality. Goldstein explains that "whatever her intentions, Madonna has made a political statement. 'Justify My Love' is wrong for MTV because it threatens the sexual order of music video. I mean the image of men as masters of street and strip" (52). Much of the fun of watching the video relies on guessing the sexuality and gender of the actors. Madonna herself has played this game on the public stage for years, in her well-advertised ambiguous relationship with Sandra Bernhard

and her excursions to lesbian bars. The fragmented quality of the music video and its many scenes suggest that
sexuality is constructed from pieces. Its performative
aspects are stressed by the attire that her partners wear
and the drawing of the moustache on one character's
face by another. This changeability gives to the music
video a compelling ambiguity. As Goldstein says, "In this
video, gender is as mutable as costume will allow, and
no one's permanently on top" (52). What gender and
sexual orientation are they? It's not clear, but that is part
of the video's message. The two characters who gaze
longingly at each other in a mirror emphasize the male
gaze and the performance of sexuality for an audience. As
in other music videos, the mirror functions to remind the
viewer of self-reflexivity: we are watching people watching people. The transformation in Madonna's appearance
makes it clear that the various sexualities are pleasurable
and that her sexual desires have been satisfied. At the
beginning of the video she is downtrodden; at the end,
she is triumphant and laughing, clearly revelling in what
she has seen and done. "The implication is that sex can
overcome the roles life sets for us, or compensate for
this tyranny by allowing men and women to play out
their dreams. Sex makes it possible to imagine a world
where the suspension of power can be hot" (Goldstein
52). Even the concluding line must be ironic: who is the
man? Is there the suggestion that women's pleasures do
not depend upon another's? In any case, the music video
clearly mixes up gender and desires in a way that points
to the complexities of the representation of sexuality.

Both En Vogue and Madonna reveal the performativity
of socially constructed gender roles, and both emphasize the possibility of women's control of sexuality. En

Vogue is more trapped in what the writer Adrienne Rich has described as compulsory heterosexuality—the closed system in which heterosexuality is presented as the only sexual option—but Madonna presents a spectrum of possibilities, including sadomasochism, homosexuality, and bisexuality. What En Vogue and Madonna have in common is the acknowledgment of the male gaze and the attempt to use it, to captivate and control it. Thus, through their use of a postmodern sensibility and style, they both expose and manipulate the notion of a male gaze.

Chapter Four

"Alternative Nation": Alternative Music, Feminism and *Beavis and Butt-Head*

The essence of the sickness in this culture that
I'd like to capture   —Courtney Love

The term "alternative music" does not refer exclusively to a specific musical style but to an attitude or positioning of a rock group. Alternative music does generally use "neopsychedelic elements over a guitar grunge and strong bass guitar/drum rhythm section" (Weinstein 79–80). But this format leaves a great deal of room for individual musical style and performance, as the music videos discussed in this chapter reveal. In certain garage or grunge band subcultures, even signing with a major record label, instead of with an "indie" or independent label, is viewed as a sellout. (The term "grunge" itself refers to the scruffy, unwashed, rebellious look sported by band members. The use of the word "garage" reflects the outsider quality of this music, bands being as likely to play in a garage as in a posh club.) Explaining the use of "alternative music" as a marketing label, Amy B. Mohan and Jean Malone write, " 'Alternative music' is used by the music media and the recording industry to categorize the work of musical groups with one or a combination of the following characteristics: unique musical styles, affiliation with an independent or non-corporate record labels and exposure through college radio and local venues rather than mainstream radio" (285).

Alternative music is specifically associated with youth subculture, in the age of its performers as well as of its audience. One of its defining events in recent years has been the Lollapalooza Festival, featuring feminist groups such as Babes in Toyland and Hole, who are discussed in this chapter. Alternative music's resistant attitude toward the corporatization of rock and roll and to traditions such as male domination has allowed feminist performers to make a place for themselves in this genre.

Mohan and Malone explain that this resistance has roots in alternative music's precursors: "Alternative music has its origins in the underground music of the 1960s and in the British punk of the 1970s, the lyrics of which stressed pessimism, alienation, and intellectual criticism of commonly held social values" (284). In her history of women in rock, *She's A Rebel,* Gillian Gaar singles out alternative music as being especially accessible to women: "In the alternative rock scene, female performers have been integrated into bands with an ease noticeably absent in the mainstream rock scene, continuing the egalitarian ethic that is the punk movement's most notable legacy" (439–40).

Alternative music reflects the postmodern era in which it has emerged. Its meshing with music videos is one aspect of alternative music's postmodernism. A wide range of alternative videos, called "Alternative Releases," was offered by a monthly video club, Rockvideo Monthly. The lyrics and images of alternative music emphasize fragmentation, especially of subjectivity, breakdown between genres, and self-reflexiveness, along with other postmodern qualities. Perhaps the most important postmodern quality of alternative music, however, is its emphasis on decentering, the lack of belief in master narratives described by Lyotard as "the postmodern condition." Female performers in alternative music draw on these postmodern aspects of the genre to create explicitly feminist messages. Alternative music performers like Courtney Love and the all-female groups Babes in Toyland, L-7, and others clearly and unambiguously identify themselves as feminists.

Courtney Love and Me'shell NdegeOcello draw on alternative music's qualities to create strong female personas and compelling feminist messages. Both work with other women—Love in her nearly all-female band, Hole, and NdegeOcello with actresses. Both stress the construction and performativity of femininity, not only in their lyrics but also in powerful music videos. Both have also achieved mainstream success with music videos featured on MTV. NdegeOcello recently had a hit duet with John Mellencamp, and she also scored a John Singleton film; the group that Love fronts, Hole, had its CD, *Live Through This,* ranked the best release of 1994 by both *Spin* and *Rolling Stone*. Hole was also featured as one of the main acts of Lollapalooza 1995, the rock festival that has now become an annual and highly prestigious music event.

Me'shell NdegeOcello is an out bisexual whose public identity shapes how viewers interpret her music videos. As she explains, "Being bisexual, black, and a woman, I have three things that make me different. . . . My songs are just stories about my life, but since I happen to be outside of what's considered normal, I've come to realize that they are political" (*Harper's Bazaar* 178). Madonna recognized and appreciated that difference and signed NdegeOcello to her own new label, Maverick. NdegeOcello draws on traditions of African-American performance such as the toast and elements of rap to create a highly unique style. Her name means "free like a bird" in Swahili (Linden 36). (The toast is an African-American tradition in which a speaker creates a rap that is based on a name and that features language play such as puns and alliteration.)

A bass guitar player, NdegeOcello crafts "If That's Your Boyfriend" around a strong bass line and her lyrics, which are counterpointed by a steady stream of spoken words by a variety of women. As NdegeOcello raps "If that's your boyfriend, he wasn't last night," she appears to taunt the other women, whose brief sentences then focus on male-female relationships, feminine subjectivity, women's roles, and competition among women. The song and music video exemplify "the tense wariness and bruised sensitivity" (*Harper's Bazaar* 178) that characterize her work. The song has been described as "tongue-in-cheek" (Linden 36), which is an apt description, as the following discussion will show.

With her close-shaven head, white sleeveless men's T-shirt, wide suspenders, and baggy pants, NdegeOcello's appearance itself calls gender into question, even for those viewers who do not know her sexual orientation. With a nose ring, a necklace, bracelets, and earrings, NdegeOcello combines elements of masculine and feminine dress in a way that is unsettling but very attractive. The other women in the cast evoke a far more traditional femininity, with a range of ethnic and feminine styles. The first face we see is an extreme close-up of a blonde woman with huge curlers in her hair, applying lipstick.

This moment evokes Annie Lennox's "Why" and a number of other feminist videos that expose the construction of femininity by showing a woman applying lipstick. As this woman and the others have their faces powdered and eye makeup applied, they talk about attracting male partners and about men cheating on them. In contrast to women in makeup ads, who are depicted as being happy about their newly altered, more feminine appearances, these female characters are desperate, and they apply makeup in a futile attempt to assuage their anguish. The makeup doesn't even withstand their anguish; they dishevel their hair, and the blonde gradually smears her lipstick all over her face. One of the women pushes her breasts up in a parody of a wonderbra, but her expression shows a grimace rather than a smile. Shot in black and white, this video, like "Independence Day," which is discussed in chapter 5, uses the absence of color to present the feel of a documentary. The bleak black-and-white footage underscores the desperation of the women's faces and their words.

In her role as the other woman, NdegeOcello exposes the other female characters' vulnerability. She appears to taunt them with her access to the boyfriend. While they are seen in extreme close-up—primarily their faces—we see NdegeOcello as an active and strong figure. She plays the bass and moves her body. In the brief shots of a guitar player and a pianist, they never show their faces directly, and it is she who controls the music and the pace. As NdegeOcello mockingly sings "ooh, baby, baby" and "good to the last drop," she parodies romantic conventions and notions of masculine sexuality. She seems to have assumed the masculine role of aggressor.

The other female characters, in contrast, play Everywoman. Their words and actions point to the construction of femininity—and it is not a pretty picture. Speaking in first person, they describe a variety of feminine plights in a male-dominated culture. The first statements raise the issue of aging "gracefully." This comment lays bare one use of cosmetics—to prey on a woman's fear of no longer being desirable to men. Women's powerlessness is also emphasized by many of the comments. The characters directly express this fear. "Sometimes I have no one to speak to and I gracefully fade into nonexistence," says one, and then another woman fills the screen and screams. This shift from language into the nonverbal evokes Julia Kristeva's notion of the preverbal feminine. In poststructuralist psychoanalyis (a la Jacques Lacan), language itself, the symbolic order, is coded as masculine. Feminine speech, then, must be completely different from our ordered symbolic system.

The fragmentation of these female characters' speech also draws attention to the masculinity of language and the impossibility of women's expressing themselves through it. The women do not speak to each other or to NdegeOcello. They do not complete their thoughts or even sentences; they continuously interrupt each other, and the camera moves abruptly from one woman's face to another's. Their subjectivity is fragmented as well. Even put together, the women's voices shatter the illusion of a unified female subject.

The viewer herself must try to make sense of the varied statements. "I felt I didn't do what he wanted and she did." "I want to be in love." "I love love." These comments all point to the dependency and vulnerability created by the idea of romance. "Oh, ok." "I'll do anything for men." "I don't need sex." These comments evoke feminine dependency on men and women's denial of their needs and their voices. One woman declares, "I need companionship," and another says, "I need a dog."

Another explains, "Once you have a child, suicide is no longer an option." Mothering is presented as another way in which women can be confined. Female laughter breaks up the morbid tone of these declarations, a laughter that evokes the feminist subversiveness of humor discussed in chapter 2. One woman says "music," another, after a pause, "video," and then "no." This phrase occurs at the very end of the song, raising the issue of how music videos are themselves implicated in the conditioning toward romance and heterosexuality that "If That's Your Boyfriend" exposes. The last sentence in the music video is "I'm not in love at all." After seeing this music video, the viewer can no longer see romantic love uncritically.

NdegeOcello repudiates romantic heterosexual love partly by her swaggering position as "the other woman," but more importantly by revealing the subordination of women through love. The song and music video contradict those music videos that champion romantic love. "If That's Your Boyfriend" reveals how romantic love separates women and makes them competitors for male attention. The only men in the music video, the other musicians, never look at the camera and are not presented as desirable. In a more serious, but still humorous, fashion, NdegeOcello makes the same point Julie Brown does in "The Homecoming Queen's Got a Gun" (discussed in chapter 2). While Brown depicts an all-white high school, NdegeOcello shows that traditional femininity handicaps both white women and black women.

The audience in Hole's music video, "Miss World," is racially diverse, but with her bleached blonde locks, Courtney Love evokes images of Marilyn Monroe and Madonna rather than of Everywoman. Love has had a high-profile and controversial life. In a story in *Vanity Fair*,

Danny Goldberg, the chairman and C. E. O. of Warner Brothers Records, says, "Courtney is emerging at a time when women in general are becoming important in rock 'n' roll, and she is the primary symbol of that" (Sessums 114). When she was married to Kurt Cobain, the lead singer for Nirvana, a tremendously succesful alternative band, Love saved his life on many occasions, including once in Europe when he took a drug overdose. When Cobain finally killed himself, Love read a letter to his gathered fans that was featured on MTV. She has been widely admired and criticized for her open expression of anger at his suicide. Before the suicide, Love had almost lost custody of her child when it was alleged that she had used heroin during her pregnancy. Featured in an MTV rockumentary as well as on the cover of *Vanity Fair,* Love is a highly visible and committed feminist. Goldberg says, "She combatively and assertively identifies herself as a feminist rock singer" (Sessums 114). Love explains, "Rock is about writing your own script; it's all about *pioneering*" (Sessums 114). Love also cites Simone de Beauvoir in the *Vanity Fair* article, and her feminism is just as clear in her music videos.

There has even been a controversy over whether Love or her friend Kat Bjelland, in the all-female group Babes in Toyland, first created the "kinderwhore" look that Love sports for her music video "Miss World." The look describes young women dressed to resemble young girls but also to look seductive. This male fantasy is here appropriated to criticize the angel/whore dichotomy that characterizes women's position in patriarchy. In a report on MTV, Kurt Loder a bit euphemistically referred to the look as "tattered baby doll image."

Live Through This, Hole's second and highly success-ful CD, reflects Love's feminism in trenchant lyrics that explicitly criticize gender roles. Like other female music video performers, Love ridicules the figure of the beauty queen for what it represents for women. "Miss World" plays off Love's celebrity as it criticizes the beauty pageant mentality and traditional femininity.

In "Miss World" Love wears a tame version of kinderwhore attire. A navy dress with a lace Peter Pan collar, short sleeves, and large white buttons falls just below her knees. She wears white knee-highs and high-heeled Mary Jane shoes with a single strap across the middle. In contrast to the childishness of the outfit is Love's bleached blonde and dishevelled hair, her bright red lipstick, a bright red heart pin, and her guitar. The bass player wears a tight white dress and black stockings; the drummer and other guitar player wear nondescript jeans and T-shirts. But the camera focuses primarily on Love, so her outfit sets the tone for the music video.

The music video opens with Love and her band playing on stage. Twinkling stars and huge letters in back spell out "Cleanliness is next to Godliness." An ironic icon, the phrase underscores the kinderwhore statement, the trite proverb evoking adjurations to children to remain clean in an unclean world. The stage is darkened, and then the spotlight strikes Love as she begins to sing. "I'm Miss World" she sings, emphasizing the fragmentation of feminine subjectivity as she immediately appears in a crowd, wearing a pale turquoise, sparkling, very lowcut gown with spaghetti straps. The music video cuts between Love's onstage image—childlike but seductive—and her passive insipid representation of a beauty queen, Miss World. As Love explains in a documentary shown on MTV, "I want to capture . . . the look on a woman's face as she's being crowned. . . . I have hemorrhoid cream under my eyes and adhesive tape on my butt and I had to scratch and claw . . . but I won Miss Congeniality. That's the essence of the sickness in this culture that I'd like to capture."

In the first cut to Love in the turquoise gown, she walks through a crowd of alternative music fans, and a young woman with cat-eye glasses places a tiara on Love's head. She covers her face with her hands, runs her hands through her hair and smiles and then staggers. She is handed a bouquet of white lilies, a symbol of innocence and virginity that represents a further mixing of contradictory images of femininity, and she wears a wrist corsage, a reference to prom night as well as to a beauty pageant. A mascara tear trickles down her cheek. The camera shows the fans parting in front of her, and then we see her back on the stage, performing in her kinderwhore outfit.

The scenes on the stage emphasize wild, passionate activity, carried out not only by Love but also by her fans. The stage performance shows how active women can and should be. On stage, she aggressively moves her body back and forth, singing and playing her guitar. We see the mosh pit with her fans wildly gyrating and slam dancing. A female fan sneaks on stage and is chased off by a security man. As Love finishes the song, she drops her guitar, knocks over the mike and leaps into the crowd, stage diving. Love shows that she is one of them and part of the action. She has demonstrated her trust and affection for the crowd by leaping into their hands. We see her Mary Jane shoes and white knee-highs as she thrusts her legs up into the air.

But the music video is not a concert video. As the music continues, we see Love attired as a beauty pageant contestant on a stage. Standing alone, she doesn't meet the camera's gaze or speak or sing. Although the words proclaim that "I am a girl who can look you in the eye," she isn't looking at us but at the ground. She drops her bouquets of flowers and stands there limp and apparently bereft.

The lyrics reveal the hollowness of the beauty pageant myth. "I'm Miss World / Somebody kill me / Kill me pills / No one cares, my friend," the song opens. "I'm Miss World / Watch me break and watch me burn / No one is listening, my friend." The refrain, which Hole's fans sing along with Love, emphasizes the loneliness and alienation of this construction of femininity. The fans' singing suggests their identification with this performance of femininity and their approval of the parody. "I made my bed, I'll lie in it / I made my bed, I'll die in it" and "I made my bed, I'll cry in it."

As in Julie Brown's "The Homecoming Queen's Got a Gun," Love exposes the anger and sadness in the role of that icon of traditional femininity, the female beauty contestant. As Brown plays the roles of the homecoming queen and of her friend, so Love plays herself, an active rock star, and Miss World. The juxtaposition of the two images of femininity makes it clear which role is more desirable, more fulfilling, more fun. Love is entertaining, energetic and active; Miss World is passive, unhappy and alienated. Like NdegeOcello, Love draws on features of postmodernism—fragmentation, especially of the subject, self-reflexivity, parody, and pastiche—to criticize traditional femininity.

Love is trying to send this feminist message to male and female rock fans, a tough sell. But Love has support in relaying this message from a seemingly unlikely source. She identifies, as Babes in Toyland and other alternative music groups do, the importance of Beavis and Butt-Head. "You've got to have the *Beavis and Butt-Head* crowd" (Sessums 114). As the following discussion of *Beavis and Butt-Head* shows, alternative music, including feminist music videos, is already a part of the show.

Beavis and Butt-Head, the animated characters who have their own show on MTV, might seem an unlikely inclusion in a book on feminist music videos. However, *Beavis and Butt-Head* frequently features alternative music, including music videos that, because they are too controversial, never make it to Rockvideo Monthly's "Alternative Releases" or to *Alternative Nation* or *Buzz Clips*, two MTV programs designed to feature such offbeat music.

Despite all the bad press they have received, the animated characters Beavis and Butt-Head deserve critical attention. This half-hour show has much to offer a feminist viewer. To use their own critical category, Beavis and Butt-Head "don't suck." The remainder of this chapter will demonstrate that *Beavis and Butt-Head* is worth analyzing, and that it has been singularly important for women in alternative music.

Its tremendous popularity alone would suggest the usefulness of an inquiry into the details of *Beavis and Butt-Head,* but the application of postmodern theory makes such a study additionally worthwhile. *Beavis and Butt-Head* is quintessentially postmodern in its use of pastiche; its questioning of subjectivity, especially the constuction of masculinity and femininity; its use of parody; its breakdown of distinction between genres (cartoon, music videos, television); and its focus on that most postmodern of contemporary forms, the music video. The show consists of the animated adventures of Beavis and Butt-Head, intercut with scenes of the two characters watching and commenting on music videos. Self-reflexivity is perhaps the most obvious of its postmodern qualities. This chapter reflects the complicated structure of the show, as the animated adventures and comments on music videos will be discussed as they appear on television, intertwined. The structure of the show as well as the music videos Beavis and Butt-Head discuss are quintessentially postmodern.

These two humorous male cartoon characters masquerade as holders of the male gaze, but in the process they expose the construction and performativity of sexuality through images. As one of the creators of Beavis and Butt-Head commented, "They're the parody of a parody of a parody" (Greenfield). Her description makes sense when we consider Beavis and Butt-Head as representations of the stereotypical MTV viewer. The antisocial and violent behavior of these two characters seems to justify the fears of Parents' Music Resource Center and of Sut Jhally in his critical video, *Dreamworlds*. Apparently working-class kids, Beavis and Butt-Head embody what their elitist critics fear music videos will produce in our youth. PRMC and Jhally are not the first to make these complaints; such criticism has long been levied at MTV, and indeed at rock and roll since its inception. So by giving a cartoon embodiment to a version of the worst stereotype of an MTV viewer, MTV is practicing what Marcuse calls "repressive tolerance," the process by which an institution incorporates criticism into its system, thus weakening and ridiculing its opposition. Tom Shales describes this action more positively: "[T]he music video channel, in business for more than a decade, finally makes a valuable social contribution: by turning on itself" (9). MTV's response to criticism is wielded in part through humor. In these extreme characters, the attacks on the deleterious effects of MTV are exaggerated and thus nullified. Beavis and Butt-Head themselves chuckle inanely through school, music videos, and life in general, but millions of viewers laugh along with them.

The opening credits make clear the distantiation that the viewer is meant to experience. Each show originally opened with the following statement:

> Beavis and Butt-Head are not real. They are stupid cartoon people completly [sic] made up by this Texas guy we hardly even know. Beavis and Butt-Head are dumb, crude, thoughtless, ugly, sexist, self-destructive fools, but for some reason the little wiener-heads make us laugh.

This introduction highlights the obvious—that these characters are not real. The criticism implicit in the adjectives "stupid, dumb, crude, ugly," and even "sexist" separates the viewer from the characters. The mention of Texas evokes another separation from MTV cool—every viewer knows MTV is urban and hip. The occasional southern accent by some of the people Beavis and Butt-Head encounter draws on a notion of southerners as separate, rural, hick. The phrase "wiener-heads" evokes the phallic emphasis in almost every episode. Despite the disclaimer, this tremendously popular new show soon produced a heated controversy, with Beavis and Butt-Head being attacked, as Bart Simpson had been before them, for presenting America's youth with negative and even dangerous messages. In one incident, *Beavis and Butt-Head* was blamed for a fire started by a five-year-old in which the child's two-year-old sister was killed (Shales

8). That the trailer where this happened was not wired for cable made no difference to those who claimed the MTV show was responsible. The moral panic resulting from this incident typifies an outdated approach to popular culture. In this Frankfurt School model, the viewer is the dupe of whatever appears on the screen. Assuming a hierarchical and patronizing tone, adults lament the corruption of the young by the media, ignoring the problems that they themselves are responsible for, such as increasing the national debt. Scapegoating popular culture provides a cheap and easy distraction from other social problems. This overly deterministic model denies the viewer any possibility of subjectivity or of any resistant way of consuming. In response to this tragedy and to the extensive attacks on the show, MTV created a new warning, moved the show from 7:00 p.m. to 10:30 p.m., and removed all references to fire from it.

The new warning reads:

> Beavis and Butt-Head are not role models. They're not even human. They're cartoons. Some of the things that they do would cause a person to get hurt, expelled, arrested, possibly even deported. To put it another way: Don't try this at home.

This revised warning still emphasizes humor, but is more directly cautionary. With only a few minor alterations, the show's premise remains the same: humor created through the antics and attitudes of two adolescent male cartoon characters. Their humor draws on the same antiauthority stance that characterizes alternative music and appeals to that music's young adult audience.

The show quickly became the most popular on MTV, and the network's ratings tripled (Greenfield). In addition, the postmodern treatment of gender and sexuality helps explain how humor can work in alternative rock music videos. *Beavis and Butt-Head*'s humor is postmodern; they transgress gender boundaries, comment on and document the fragmentation of the self, and evoke self-reflexiveness through references to music videos, cartoons, and television history. What is most important from a feminist perspective, however, is that *Beavis and Butt-Head* provides a place for women performers of alternative music and their feminist messages.

The impact of *Beavis and Butt-Head* can hardly be overestimated. As a *Rolling Stone* cover story on the two characters proclaimed, "50,000,000 Beavis and Butt-Head Fans Can't Be Wrong." In that article, Charles Young also describes Beavis and Butt-Head as "the most powerful critics in rock and roll." With a simple lexicon, Beavis and Butt-Head "were able to put lesser-known bands like White Zombie and Babes in Toyland on the map with a single word (cool) and destroy established acts with another (sucks)" (39). A case study of their effect on the fortunes of one band (Babes in Toyland) illustrates the show's ability to make or break acts. It is well known that MTV itself helped pull a declining record industry out of a severe slump by generating new interest and new audiences for albums. As the most popular show on MTV, *Beavis and Butt-Head* has the same power to affect individual groups. The playlist for *Beavis and Butt-Head* demonstrates a much wider range than the videos played on any other show, or on MTV or VH-1 generally. Beavis and Butt-Head watch alternative videos, old videos, odd videos, even country music videos. The episode with Babes in Toyland illustrates their power to bring eclectic cult groups, especially those with feminist messages, to national and international fame.

Despite all the promotional material and phone calls made to MTV by Warner executives, Babes in Toyland's first video, "Bruise Violet" only aired once, on Sunday night at midnight. But without any promotion at all, "Bruise Violet" appeared on *Beavis and Butt-Head*. Not only did it air, but Beavis and Butt-Head loved the video. Because *Beavis and Butt-Head* shows are run many times, "Bruise Violet" ran on MTV for several months. Neal Karlen wrote that "Babes in Toyland received one of the most positive reviews that Beavis and Butt-Head had ever given" (276). The Babes drummer, Lori, knew what it meant to receive approval from Beavis and Butt-Head. "Beavis and Butt-Head said we don't even suck?" she asked. "Beavis and Butt-Head love us? I guess we've arrived!" (Karlen 276). Their CD had sold a meagre fifty thousand copies before the video began playing on *Beavis and Butt-Head*. By the time the particular episode was banned because of a reference to fire, their sales had reached almost two hundred thousand.

What is even more remarkable about this story is that Beavis and Butt-Head had promoted a band considered a feminist band, an all-female rock band that presents a feminine perspective. Part of a movement known as Riot Grrrls, Babes in Toyland belong to "that loose network of hard-rocking girl bands and their fans dedicated to the feminist manifesto 'Revolution girl-style Now!' . . . Although not officially affiliated with the movement, [Babes in Toyland] were claimed as patron saints by the young women who had recently turned rock and roll played by women into a political issue" (Karlen 12–13). Their video features Cindy Sherman, an important feminist artist, playing the lead singer Kat's doppelganger. The images of Kat screaming "liar!," and applying and smearing her lipstick, emphasize the construction and performance of femininity. The promotion of this video on *Beavis and Butt-Head* is but one example of the ways in which the show defies critics of its sexism. The show's representation and treatment of gender is actually more open and challenging than that of the regular MTV playlist, or indeed of television shows in general.

Another instance of the complication of gender roles on *Beavis and Butt-Head* is the depiction of sexual harassment. Again, the airing of another offbeat video on the show demonstrates the ways in which Beavis and Butthead are used as foils rather than as role models. Maggie Estep appears in very brief segments as part of MTV's *Spoken Word* series. On *Beavis and Butt-Head*, however, she is given much more time—we see her entire video.

As we saw in chapter 2, in "Hey Baby," Estep tackles the issue of sexual harassment directly and radically. The video shows her walking down a street, being followed and harassed by an exaggeratedly creepy man. As he harasses her, she protests, and then finally turns around to attack him. The video depicts a role reversal, and there are also images of men hanging on meat hooks, men with "choice" and "stupid" stamped on them as if they were meat. As Estep says in the video, "I don't have anything against men, just stupid men." This music video, explicitly feminist and quite radical, got virtually no airplay on MTV. By including it, *Beavis and Butt-Head* again demonstrates a flexibility and openness that is remarkable. The show provides a place for alternative visions such as Estep's radical feminist critique of sexual harassment.

Of course, the characters Beavis and Butt-Head completely misunderstand the meaning of the video. Here irony works to unite *Beavis and Butt-Head*'s creator with the viewer. Beavis and Butt-Head so completely misinterpret the situation, even to the point of misreading words on the screen, that the viewer takes pleasure in the absurdity of their errors. Their voiceover reveals that they identify with the creepy sexual harasser. The viewer, however, is situated in a superior position: we see the video, and our laughter stems in part from Beavis and Butt-Head's misreading. As in all the shows, we are encouraged to feel superior to Beavis and Butt-Head, just as Estep is superior to the loutish harasser who follows her.

In two other brief animated segments, Beavis and Butt-Head underscore the stupidity of sexual harassment. One clip shows Beavis and Butt-Head watching a group of construction workers harassing a woman who walks by on a sidewalk. The workers make rude comments, and she rebukes them sarcastically. In the sequence with the construction workers, Beavis and Butt-Head are impressed by the workers' harassment of women. Butt-Head comments, "Those guys are cool," and Beavis agrees—"They know how to talk to girls." As the woman's scornful response to the harassers shows, the construction workers don't know how to talk to girls, because women respond harshly and dismissively to those kinds of overtures. Beavis and Butt-Head inadvertently expose the sexually exploitative nature of many music videos when Butt-Head suggests that "they [the construction workers] should do a video." There immediately follows a music video featuring two female groups, Salt 'n Pepa and En Vogue, all scantily clad, singing "whatta man." This video emphasizes the distorted representation of femininity in women wild with sexual desire, and Beavis plaintively asks as he watches Salt 'n Pepa gyrate, "How come chicks are only horny like that on TV?" The answer, obviously, is that what we see on TV is only a construction. In another example that exposes sexual harassment, we see the consequences of this sexist attitude toward women when Butt-Head accosts a woman at a bus stop. Both Beavis and Butt-Head are thoroughly trounced for their transgression. The woman blows a whistle, and a nearby guard runs out, grabs Beavis and Butt-Head by their ankles, and slams them into the sidewalk. These moments from the show reveal that sexual harassment is not fun or rewarding but in fact is ridiculous and disgusting.

Other animated sequences detail a postmodern and complicated representation of gender. In "Sporting Goods," Beavis and Butt-Head are sent by their gym teacher, a formidable and stupid macho man, to get jockstraps. Their classmate Daria has just had her gender role defined for her, having been assigned the job of fashion reporter "just because she is a girl." She undertakes the job reluctantly, but is rewarded when her path crosses with Beavis and Butt-Head's. Daria is a character never mentioned in critiques of the show, but she is a smart young woman who frequently catches and exposes Beavis and Butt-Head at their most inane moments.

In this sequence, Beavis and Butt-Head attempt to purchase jockstraps, but even the smallest size is too large. They go into a dressing room—together—to try on eye patch protectors. They emerge, lifting their T-shirts to reveal the eye patch protectors as jockstraps—and Daria snaps their picture for the school paper.

This episode reveals the paucity of definitions of masculinity. Beavis and Butt-Head find themselves in a role reversal as Daria captures the two male voyeurs with her camera—an inversion of the standard male gaze, in which women's bodies are captured for a male viewer's pleasure. Laura Mulvey has detailed the ways in which this gaze functions in classic Hollywood cinema to force the viewer into a masculine subject position. Here, on MTV, *Beavis and Butt-Head* creates a postmodern reversal. Daria is in a position to comment on them, and their picture makes the front page of the school paper. At the same time, there are clues to Beavis and Butt-Head's homosociality as they share a dressing room even though another stands empty. They are always together and rarely with girls. The contradictions in adolescent male sexuality are repeatedly exposed, both in the characters' animated adventures and in the music videos they watch.

The freakish nature of adolescent male sexuality is emphasized in "Carnival," where again Beavis and Butt-Head start out as spectators but end up as subjects. In an adventure that Foucault would have loved, Beavis and Butt-Head go to a carnival and see freaks. The first freak that they see advertised is a "half man/half woman," who illustrates (as the hermaphrodite Hercule Barbin did for Foucault) the indecipherability and constructiveness of gender. As the hawker claims, this creature was "born with two perfect functioning sets of gender organs. Folks, he's never lonely on Saturday night." Beavis and Butt-Head then go in to see the Rubber Band Lady, whose skill is to contort her body into various unnatural positions. Thrilled by her performance, Beavis and Butt-Head go backstage. There the Rubber Band Lady solicits them, thinking that they have come to seek her out for sex. But they are slow to respond and are thrown out, at which point they join the circus themselves as Siamese twins, their T-shirts sewn together. This conversion suggests once again that the puerile adolescent sexuality that they represent is somehow as freakish and as artificial as the carnival acts.

Similarly, in another episode about gender and performance, Beavis and Butt-Head practice with each other for mudwrestling with "girls" they see on TV. Of course, they never make it to mudwrestle with actual women. Instead, as they practice with each other, wearing bikini tops and rolling around in the mud, Daria again captures them in a moment of vulnerability. This homosocial depiction is not used to denigrate the male characters but to point to the ways in which masculinity is focused around relations with other males.

These vignettes reveal that *Beavis and Butt-Head* is much more complex than most media critics acknowledge. These examples of the depiction of sexual harassment and homosociality provide specific instances of the show's complexity. But there are many other ways in which the postmodern aspects of the show provide viewers with the opportunity to critique our culture, especially adolescent male culture. *Beavis and Butt-Head* complicate ideas about gender and gender roles. The show is self-reflexive; Beavis and Butt-Head function both as viewers and as critics of music videos. They are continually looking for videos that "don't suck," a category incorporated into another MTV show in which the human VJs promised viewers "videos that don't suck" (the show's title). *Beavis and Butt-Head* consists of brief animated segments of the two characters' adventures, such as those described, punctuated by scenes of them watching videos and channel surfing. As they cruise the channels, they comment on the music videos. They are primarily interested in music videos that involve demolition, fire and "babes." In their elemental search for the perfect music video, Beavis and Butt-Head reveal the misogyny of many music videos. Their expression of the crass desire for the titillation of sex and destruction makes us aware of our own participation in that search, even though it may occur to a much smaller degree. The characters' focus on any mention of sexuality, no matter how remote or unintentional, emphasizes the absurdity of viewing sex in isolation from all other aspects of human existence.

Beavis and Butt-Head also exposes the exploitation that underlies advertising and music videos insofar as they function as ads. As they watch a music video performed by Siouxsie and the Banshees, Butt-Head asks a rhetorical question—"How does this chick expect to sell records without showing cleavage?" The question makes the viewer laugh, but it also raises the issue of sexism in rock marketing. Discussions of music videos in Lisa A. Lewis's *Gender Politics and MTV* and in articles I have published indicate that it is possible to sell CDs without showing cleavage. Butt-Head's comment, exposing the environment in which music videos are marketed and consumed, reveals and ridicules this type of exploitation of women's bodies.

If Beavis and Butt-Head can channel surf looking for what they see as desirable qualities, then so can other viewers. They are a model of a viewer in control of what appears, not its slave. They also present us with the possibility of choice. Not surprisingly, very few music videos live up to Beavis and Butt-Head's desires. They almost never watch a music video all the way through. Furthermore, their show contains more outré, offbeat and alternative music videos than any other MTV show, even *Alternative Nation*. Beavis and Butt-Head watch many music videos that directly challenge their own traditional and narrowly expressed view of sexuality. Almost every show reveals a challenge to the dominant sexual order, and their adventures similarly produce challenges to gender roles.

An examination of four music videos and Beavis and Butt-Head's reaction to them demonstrates the ways in which postmodernism affects the depiction of gender. The music videos, which all comment on traditional gender roles, the fragmentation of the self, and sexuality, represent the type of alternative offbeat music video that the two characters watch—the type conspicuously absent from other music video channels and shows.

In three separate shows, Beavis and Butt-Head watched "I Wish You Were a Beer" by Cycle Sluts from Hell, "Heterosexual Man" by the Odds, "Who Was in My Room Last Night?" by the Butthole Surfers, and "Bikini Girls with Machine Guns" by the Cramps. As each of these music videos is from a band at the fringe (only the Butthole Surfers have any large national following), these examples support the contention made concerning Babes in Toyland—that the Beavis and Butt-Head show broadens MTV's sometimes narrow and repetitive playlist. *Beavis and Butt-Head* also provides a space where sexuality and gender roles can be dealt with explicitly through humor.

Like "Bruise Violet," "I Wish You Were a Beer" by the Cycle Sluts From Hell, an all-female band, also meets Beavis and Butt-Head's criteria: it is cool. With their leather attire and rough posturing, the Cycle Sluts are a female heavy metal band, strong and somewhat frightening. They make fun of groupies and traditional gender roles by asking, "Are you with the band?" when they are the band, and bellowing "You look good." Instead of a good time with a man, they are telling the men they prefer beer, a role reversal in which women spurn men, taking control of a stereotype of macho behavior. The band's name and their parody of gender roles make it clear again that in music videos, and presumably in rock and roll, there is space for playing with traditional sexual roles.

"Heterosexual Man" by the Odds might seem at first to describe exactly the role that Beavis and Butt-Head seek. They certainly think so, agreeing at once that this video is cool, and that they would like to go to a bar and drink with these guys. "I wanna make every woman I see" begins the song, and certainly PRMC and Sut Jhally would be appalled by this lyric. But the music and video are more complicated than these opening words suggest. Indeed the very insistence on being heterosexual draws attention to heterosexuality as a construction, and it is a construction that starts slipping as the video unfurls. A male character goes into the bathroom and slicks back his hair; then, as he looks again, to his horror he sees his own face feminized. Shocked, he looks back again, to be reassured by his masculine visage. As he walks out into the bar, the band performing "Heterosexual Man" begins a transformation. One by one, the band members appear dressed in women's clothes, wearing pearls and make-up, their hair coifed in traditional feminine styles. Then the band members lose their clothes, and it becomes difficult to see what gender they are. At this point Beavis becomes excited by their ostensible nudity and directs Butt-Head's attention to the screen. The two argue about whether there are men or women on the television screen. Neither Beavis nor Butt-Head quite figures out what is happening, but the viewer cannot escape the gender-bending going on.

Similarly, "Who Was in My Room Last Night?" by the Butthole Surfers presents a male character unsure of who was in his bed the previous night. The lyrics are accompanied by animation that depicts a strong and powerful female character rapaciously attacking a male character. Their nudity suggests sexual intercourse, and, after the female throws him up in the air, the male character runs from her terrified. Another scene shows a woman with red hair placing a pair of panties over a male driver's head, causing him to lose control of the car. At the same time, a young innocent girl with red hair is shown roller-skating with a lollipop; an ambulance runs over her and flips upside down. The girl stands there unhurt. These sequences all suggest the power of feminine sexuality to disrupt and dis-order. The male character wakes up in the hospital with a red-haired nurse lasciviously licking a lollipop. She licks her lips and then leans over the man, who is bundled up in bandages, with one leg suspended, helpless. This image of female sexual desire—the suggestion that the female character is able and willing to pursue such desire—is presented as strong and perhaps intimidating.

The campy 1950s titles in another music video are postmodern and parodic. "Bikini Girls with Machine Guns" by the Cramps is another example of a video that draws our attention to female sexuality and makes fun of it. The music video is framed by "Heroes," an adventure in which Beavis and Butt-Head buy guns. They see a trailer for *Cops*, a television show featuring the shooting of an innocent man by police, followed by an ad for "Bob's Fancy Skeet," a gun shop. Butt-Head comments, "Wow! Guns are cool," and then the Cramps' music video begins. It opens with a turbaned figure making the pronouncement "All things are possible . . . ," and then he declares, "All things that are knowable will be realized in this new dimension of bikini girls with machine guns." This apparent non sequitur is interrupted by the appearance of the title "The Cramps in Bikini Girls With Machine Guns." While the music video meets with Beavis and Butt-Head's approval—"If only all videos could be like this!" says Butt-Head—the music video is more complicated than it appears to them. Like other music videos shown on *Beavis and Butt-Head*, this video employs images and song to comment on representations of female sexuality. The juxtaposition of bikini girls with machine guns is absurd and points to our culture's fascination with weapons and violence and its exploitation of female sexuality. The neon signs that form the backdrop for the bikini girls are reminiscent of the signs that appear in explicitly feminist videos such as Annie Lennox's "Why" or Salt 'n Pepa's "Shoop" and have the same effect. The signs, which read "girls, girls, girls," "hostess—cocktails" and "star," remind the viewer of the commodification of the female body. The bikini girls are a reference to Miss America and other beauty pageant contestants. One bikini girl sports a red-and-white polka dot bikini and sits on top of a slowly turning table; there is a blue background with white stars. The patterns suggest the American flag. The bikini girl wears a tiara, and, as the table turns, she waves her hand as Miss America does. Like Julie Brown's "The Homecoming Queen's Got a Gun," this video, by juxtaposing violence and the depiction of woman as trophy or sexual object, makes the point that femininity is a construction. Humor further emphasizes this point, as one bikini girl slowly pulls out a wad of gum, and another waves two bombs close to her breasts. This ludicrous juxtaposition reminds the viewer of the all-too-real glamorization of physical violence in connection with sex in ads and pornography. The other band members' attire reinforces the notion of gender and, by implication, of sexual desire, as a construction. The male vocalist wears a shiny plastic body suit and patent leather high heels, while the female bass player is modestly attired in a plain dress, her hair up in a bun. This type of humorous music video problematizing sexuality frequently appears on *Beavis and Butt-Head*; these four are especially prominent since Beavis and Butt-Head watch them all the way through, a rare occurrence.

But the depiction and parodying of the male gaze are found not only in the music videos but also in Beavis and Butt-Head's animated adventures. In "Naked Colony," for example, Beavis and Butt-Head crash a nudist colony. They spend all day staring at the naked people, chuckling repeatedly by the end of the day. Then in a pseudo-news report entitled "40 Years Later," Beavis and Butt-Head are interviewed by a reporter and asked about the highlight of their lives. Butt-Head replies "seeing naked people" and they both chuckle. Placed in this perspective, seeing naked people is reduced to the most meaningful goal of a meaningless life.

Throughout their adventures, Beavis and Butt-Head make sexual jokes and puns. They are continually playing with sexual innuendo about tools such as fishing rods and chainsaws. In one brief sketch, Beavis uses a chain saw to cut off the head of a grasshopper, cutting off, at the same time, the tip of Butt-Head's finger, clearly an act of symbolic castration, a kind of threat and response to the characters' sexual desires and their misdirection. Mike Judge, one of the creators of Beavis and Butt-Head, places Daria, their smart female classmate, in a position to catch them in ridiculous postures and to make withering commentaries on their sexual desires and behaviors. In "Scared Straight," the characters' homosocial attraction to each other and their ambiguous gender situation are stressed when they are called Beaver and Butt-Hole by the prisoners in the jail they are visiting. Daria's commentaries, the extreme absurdity of the characters, and the music videos they watch all constitute a critique of the male gaze and of traditional depictions of sexuality.

Significantly, this criticism is deftly wielded through postmodernism. The show's fragmented nature, its emphasis on representation (two cartoon characters commenting on filmed videos), and the self-reflexiveness of the viewer observing two cartoon characters watching music videos as he or she also watches these videos make the show emblematically postmodern. And, not surprisingly, the music videos the characters watch also draw on postmodernism's tenets: breakdown between genres, the fragmented self, disbelief in master narratives, parody, and pastiche to criticize sexism. *Beavis and Butt-Head*'s critique of sexual harassment is reminiscent of the directness of the alternative music performed by Courtney Love and Me'shell NdegeOcello. Alternative music and its fans provide explicit challenges to traditional gender mores.

Chapter Five

"Independence Day": Feminist Country Music Videos

Hey Cinderella—does the shoe fit you now?
—Suzy Bogguss

The preceding chapters on postmodernism, humor, sexuality and alternative music provide the backdrop for our consideration in the final three chapters of feminist music videos in particular genres. Such case studies deserve attention, for both country music, discussed in this chapter, and rap, discussed in chapters 6 and 7, provide examples of feminist performances in genres traditionally considered almost innately misogynist. As country music is historically a rural-centered music performed almost exclusively by European-Americans, rap has an urban focus and is created almost entirely by African-American performers. A discussion of country music and of rap enables us to see the ways in which the feminism of the performers provides commonality. The fact that rap is seen as racially typed in a negative way, when its fans are both European-American and African-American, while country music is not regarded as being similarly restricted, shows the degree to which popular culture produced by European-American subcultures is still considered racially unmarked. Some country music critics and performers even connect the rise in country music's popularity to listener rejection of rap.[1]

While country music and rap may seem to have little in common, female music video performers in both genres use the qualities of postmodernism to create feminist messages. Fragmentation, the breakdown between genres, critique of master narratives, and an examination of female subjectivity characterize feminist music videos in both genres. Also, performers in both country music and rap use specific features of their genres in crafting feminist messages for mass audiences.

Country music's recent surge in popularity also merits critical attention, and there is more involved than a rejection of rap. As Cecelia Tichi cogently argues, country music should not be seen or dismissed as a marginal or regional genre. That she feels compelled to demonstrate country music's innate Americanness shows that its national qualities are in question even in 1994.[2] By a number of measures, country music's popularity has increased dramatically.[3] The generalizations that explain country music's popularity, however, do not necessarily apply to the extremely successful women performers. For example, Susan Holly says that "theories abound to explain the current country craze. The popular wisdom is that Americans are turning back to hearth and home for comfort in sober economic times" (34). Such an explanation, however, does not acknowledge the radical critiques of hearth and home made by female country music performers. Furthermore, figures suggest that the audience for country music is predominantly female: Paul Kingsbury cites a study showing that the purchasers of country music are 54 percent women and 46 percent men (1992c, 24). Kingsbury goes on to claim that "country music is enjoying an unprecedented flowering of women's music. Never before in the history of country music have so many women artists sold so many records so consistently" (20–21). He explains this development by arguing that "country music has always reflected America's values. The goals of the women's liberation movement may have taken hold more gradually in the heartland than they did in media capitals, but those values have now filtered down into music. Just as in all other walks of American life, women are no longer just standing by the men in country music" (21). Kingsbury's explanation is persuasive, but, perhaps unfairly, he depicts country music as being regressive or slow to reflect social change. Nevertheless, country music's popularity and the success of women performers justify the discussion in this book (see also Bufwack and Oermann 388; Rogers 20; Howell 108).

Country music may seem an unlikely ally of feminism, since stereotypically it includes the idea of profound conservatism. It is a stereotype reinforced by the suffering victim routine played by some famous country female performers, most notably Tammy Wynette, whose famous song "Stand by Your Man" depicts a woman subordinating herself to her man. The song was even featured prominently in the 1992 presidential election when Hillary Rodham Clinton declared that she was not a "stand by your man" kind of woman (Kingsbury 1992c, 21). Clinton was using the title as shorthand to refer to oppressed women. As Simon Frith maintains, this common interpretation is overly simplistic. And country music has always had a place for strong, assertive women performers, as Mary Bufwack and Robert Oermann's recent book, *Finding Her Voice: The Saga of Women in Country Music*, amply demonstrates (see also Banes). That tradition continues to grow stronger and stronger, and its evolution can be traced in country music videos. Unfortunately, some recent texts about country music, such as Cecelia Tichi's otherwise excellent study, *High Lonesome*, fail to recognize this phenomenon. And while Bufwack and Oermann's overview of women and country music is exciting and comprehensive, their volume spends little time exploring a recent and exciting development for women—feminist country music videos.

As has happened in other musical genres, music videos have changed the presentation and appeal of country music (see Fenster 113 for a discussion of the development of country music videos). The two music video channels reach over 70 million households, and are rapidly growing in popularity (Painton 65). While, as I will argue, music videos and the two country music channels, The Nashville Network (TNN) and Country Music Television (CMT), have provided access for female performers, an examination of the genre and its history also helps to explain why, once music videos were created, women were able to move in so quickly to take advantage of this new form. I will further show how certain country music videos contain what Joan Radner and Susan Lanser describe as "feminist messages—that is, messages critical of some aspects of women's subordination" (3).

This notion of feminist messages is crucial to understanding and appreciating the kinds of feminism present in country music. Academic critics especially must learn not to look for reflections of how an intellectual or theorist would produce a subversive message. Popular songs and videos have quite a different task, a broader one—to raise the issue of women's subordination and to expose sexism in an entertaining and nonthreatening fashion to a mass audience. Consequently, the types of feminism found in country music videos, like the feminism in other music videos, are frequently indirect or specifically focused rather than overtly didactic or tendentious.

The generic qualities of country music lend themselves to feminist appropriation. As in a very different genre, rap, lyrics are of preeminent importance to a country music song. There is frequently clever word play, including puns, which requires the listener to pay close attention. If you are choosing a genre in which to get a message across, one that emphasizes words is perfect. In addition to the emphasis on diction, country music lyrics often relate a narrative, which has been a staple of feminist protest since the Victorian era. The music lends itself as well to appropriation by those on the margins of the genre. While country music sounds vary, and some, like the famous Nashville sound created by Chet Atkins, require a great deal of technology, the basic instruments of country music (a guitar, a fiddle) are cheap and easily accessible. Many female country music performers, like Loretta Lynn, were able to start with just a guitar. While the inexpensive equipment makes country music available to both men and women, it is women, who historically have made less money and had less access to capital and education, who have benefitted more.

Two other qualities of country music render it susceptible to feminist appropriation: its content and its style. Country music songs most frequently focus on relationships and emotions, areas of central concern to women and an important source of women's oppression.[4] Since country music was already committed to this discussion, women performers can express from a woman's point of view their concerns about love and how love is used against them. Finally, the most commonly discussed characteristic of country music—its sincerity or "heart"—makes it suitable as a place where feminist performers can raise feminist issues in a very personal and direct fashion. While it is true that this aura of authenticity is constructed, and is quite clearly a performance, it nonetheless simulates sincerity and direct address. Here I disagree with Barbara Ching, who argues that "once country music is seen as a form of cultural representation and critique, the question of 'authenticity' should seem irrelevant" (117). Her insightful essay may apply to the male performers she discusses, but the feminist performances I consider rely on the notion of authenticity. Pam Tillis, a performer examined in some detail later in this chapter, insists that "if you're a woman, you sing about your real experience and people gonna know it's the truth" (Kingsbury 1992c, 30). As critic Jimmie Rogers writes, "A country music song is treated as a special form of communication—communication that more closely resembles interpersonal or face-to-face interaction between two people than do other types of mass appeal music" (x). If the country music performer succeeds in convincing the audience of her sincerity, she may persuade them to consider or accept new or unfamiliar attitudes, such as feminism. Without considering feminism, Rogers claims, "The [country music] audience will accept the source's attitudes—as long as the source appears to approach the sentiment honestly" (230). This "sincerity contract" may explain the success of many feminist country music performers, especially early ones like Loretta Lynn. As Ching says about country music, "The singers and listeners are *acting* naturally, and *naturally,* they're acting" (122). Most importantly, women performers are acting naturally *successfully.*

Lynn and other women performers certainly needed the "sincerity contract" and whatever other skills they could use to combat the conservatism and sexism of the country music world. While a few strong and assertive female performers left a legacy to be realized in the 1980s and 1990s, only a few were very successful. Perhaps the rarity of successful women is one of the reasons that today's women country music performers cherish the female country music singers of the previous genera-tions. In no other musical genre do today's performers seem so appreciative of those who paved the way. This appreciation is shown in many references, and, more important, in collaborations among different generations of performers. The television special discussed at the end of this chapter, "The Women of Country," also reveals the importance of country music foremothers to the current generation.

Before 1955, as Bufwack and Oermann explain, "New female stars were rare" (169). Part of the problem, as they identify it, was the entrenched conservatism of Nashville, which became the dominant center of the country music business. "It was a cruel irony for women that this industry settled in Nashville, for no southern city is so hidebound by conservative religion" (180). In his massive tome, *Country Music, U.S.A.: Revised Edition,* Bill Malone states that "country music songs, then, fre-quently exude compassion, but are rarely liberal in any conventionally defined sense" (300). Malone concludes that "country music's political stance remained difficult to characterize" (374). While I agree that it is difficult to characterize the stance of an entire genre, it is possible to identify the politics and success of feminist country music performers. Malone mentions female performers only briefly, and his critical neglect of them runs the danger of contributing to the conservatism he describes.

Unfortunately, the response of many critics to both country music and country music videos has been to dismiss them as merely and consistently misogynist. In contrast, my analysis allows the contributions of female performers to be highlighted. Like much of popular culture, especially advertisements, country music videos have been seen to objectify women. While it is true that many country music videos, such as "God Bless Texas," which features several bikini-clad women, depict women in a degrading fashion, music videos are not inherently sexist or oppressive. Nor is country music, and neither genre deserves the quick and easy dismissal that has been the reaction of many feminists to both.

Acknowledging the performative aspects of country music enables my reading of the presence of resistance in country music videos. As I argue in chapter 1, looking at music videos from a poststructuralist view allows us to see the moments when women are able to resist the misogyny and oppression so prevalent in popular culture. Poststructuralism licenses the reading of the body and performance as legitimate texts and allows us to look beyond traditional sexist notions of authorship to see that female performers are also authors of the video texts. If we accept that feminist country music stars are performing authenticity and sincerity, we can give them credit for a successful (conscious or unconscious) strategy of persuasion.

The star-centered institution of music videos further empowers the performer. Information on music video directors is difficult to obtain, while every video carries the name of its star, and Video Hit One's country programming, for example, emphasizes the primacy of the star. On VH-1, the credits acknowledge the performer, the song title, the CD title, the record company, and the director, in that order. On TNN, the song title appears first, followed by the performer's name, the CD title, and the songwriter's name(s). In any case, music videos are perceived to belong to the star because it is her visage that the viewer sees. Poststructuralist theory encourages the discussion of the performer as an equal participant, another voice, rather than as the puppet of a director. The performer's tone, gestures, and lyrics, in many cases written by her, strongly determine what will be presented in the video. While all music videos, then, have the potential to be liberating for women, there are significant differences among music videos by women, even those that can be described as feminist. This chapter will explore a range of strategies that are not more or less feminist, but which approach the communication of a feminist message from different perspectives. What is important for academics to realize is that the constraints of a mass market form like music videos do not necessarily dilute a feminist message, but instead expand its receivership to millions of viewers, male and female, who would not describe themselves as feminist. Issues of purity are quite simply inappropriate in terms of feminism in country music.

While differing in styles and approaches to feminist ideas, the three feminist country music videos and the television special discussed in this chapter all share an attention to the oppression of women. The three videos are but a small sample of a large number of feminist music videos. In *Hot Country Women*, Mike Kosser discusses over twenty female country music performers, explaining that "[t]hese women have not only helped revolutionize the status of women in country music. They have also helped change the attitudes of those who listen to country music" (2). In a period of less than two months' casual viewing, my colleague, Jerry Martin, collected thirty feminist country music videos.[5] Those that are discussed here are representative of the variety of approaches that female performers take. Humor is one common approach, and Pam Tillis's "Cleopatra, Queen of Denial" reveals how humor can be used to present a powerful but nonthreatening feminist message. Tillis's video typifies country music's clever appropriation of language for a feminist message. She draws upon postmodernism's use of humor, the sense of a fragmented self, and self-reflexiveness. A second approach is to expose romantic myths, and Suzy Bogguss's "Hey Cinderella" responds to the fairy tale narratives that mislead and confine women. Her narrative involves women of all ages, from a young girl to the fairy godmother, and rejects the message of feminine dependence. Featuring a strongly postmodern style, this music video suggests the impossibility of the female self living under the guidelines of a master narrative of romance. Some feminist music videos, direct and explicit, are clearly didactic; Martina McBride's "Independence Day" is a brutal exposé of domestic violence, told from the point of view of the battered woman's daughter. In this story, social acceptance of battering and the battered woman's resistance are presented in haunting images and words. Drawing on a pastiche of images from a small-town Independence Day celebration, the music video fragments the unified narrative of the lyrics. Finally, the solidarity present in "The Women of Country," a television special that features more than sixty-five women country music performers, demonstrates the sense of sisterhood that marks country music feminism.

Pam Tillis comes by her country music heritage directly; she is the daughter of Mel Tillis, the "country king named Entertainer of the Year in 1976" (Bufwack and Oermann 546). Tillis first performed at the Grand Ole Opry at the age of eight, but she tried many other musical forms before returning to country in 1986. She has performed at benefits for the Nashville Women's Shelter, and comments on the roles for women in country music: "I just don't think women are as ready to go for their old stereotypes. They are not following the old patterns. What are the stereotypes for rock 'n' roll? Sex vixen? Country women aren't into doing that" (548). Her music synthesizes her political interests, and she uses humor to make a feminist message entertaining as well as compelling.

Tillis draws upon a long-standing convention of country music, humor, especially word play such as punning, a practice for which her father is well known. Pam's humor, however, is most decidedly feminist, especially when compared to examples of her father's, which includes an elaborate routine about Dolly Parton's breasts. This change reflects a shift in country music humor and the uses to which it is put. Don Cusic identifies it as a move from the comic routine—such as the one about Parton's body—to the comic song. He says that "as comedy became less a matter of doing a comic routine or skits in a live show, the humorous song began to play an important role for performers" (46). Pam Tillis puts the humorous song to quite serious use. Again Cusic identifies this change without identifying feminists: "The humor itself may change with the times" (50). As discussed in chapter 2, humor itself is deconstructive and powerful.

Humor can be used to make trenchant criticisms of patriarchal society. Feminist humor is aggressive, disturbing, disruptive. Because humor is aggressive, "the humorist adopts at least a *stance* of superiority, a position of privileged insight" (Walker 25). Through humor, an audience can be manipulated into seeing or at least laughing at gender stereotypes or patriarchal conventions. Laughter can rupture the illusion of patriarchal authority and imperviousness. Most important, humor can make a feminist message appealing to a wide audience. In part because of their energetic optimism about the possibility of change, these feminist country music videos suggest that humor can be a particularly effective tool in the arena of popular culture.

The clever and humorous visual style of Tillis's music video makes it clear that it is unequal gender roles and "queens of denial" who are being satirized in the song. While the music video is cute and appealing, Tillis uses this style for a serious purpose; as Nancy Walker and other feminist critics of humor have suggested, women's humor is "a very serious thing." Tillis exposes and criticizes the ways in which women encourage, apologize for, and excuse male philandering and lying. The male figure for whom the Queen continually makes excuses is not particularly attractive: with his big black cowboy hat and white sleeveless T-shirt, he is a caricature of a country boy. He mugs and makes faces at other women right in front of the singer. Meanwhile, the singer is surrounded by attractive male figures only too willing to wait upon her; yet her obsession with this man causes her to ignore the other possibilities. Tillis is attired in a short white dress with cowboy boots, and her hair and the set evoke notions of Egyptian splendor with touches of country. This juxtaposition itself is humorous, but it also contains the idea that at one time women, as queens, did have some power, although, even for someone like Cleopatra, it could be undercut by love. "Just call me Cleopatra, everybody, cause I'm the Queen of Denial" runs the refrain. "Queen of Denial, buying all his alibis / Floating down a river of lies."

The critique of contemporary culture is made explicit as the singer reads a series of self-help books with titles like *Women Who Hate Men Who Hate Women* and *I'm OK—You're a Jerk*, both titles that apply to the Queen's situation. At the end of the video, the books seem to have helped—Tillis throws one at her paramour's picture, and his visage changes from a smirk to a look of dismay as the framed portrait falls over. The Queen of Denial has learned her lesson, a lesson that has been reinforced by a trio of backup singers in a beauty shop, cotton balls between their freshly painted toenails. The attention to female rites of beauty underscores the wasted attention spent on an unappreciative and unworthy male, an approach identified by Radner and Lanser in folk culture as "Barbara Babcock's notion of *symbolic inversion* and Luce Irigaray's concept of *mimicry*, in which a patriarchally designated feminine position is repeated with exaggeration in order to expose it" (10). The music video stresses the postmodern sense of a fragmented, artificial self that is a construction. Femininity is revealed as a performance.

The music video explicitly draws attention to the idea of performance in one sequence where two characters in Egyptian attire pull back a curtain to reveal Tillis, dressed in black leather pants and jacket, singing into a microphone. Her backup singers appear first in the pink-and-gold beauty shop, and then in gold cover-ups with masks over their faces. This set emphasizes the performance of femininity and recovers Tillis not just as the Queen of Denial (Queen of the Nile) but as a performer singing about this type of trap for women. Tillis's role as a leader and critic is emphasized as she directs her backup singers and others in a country line dance with an Egyptian flavor. Further, Tillis's dramatic hand gestures—reminiscent of silent film acting—her facial grimaces, and her tone of voice reveal to the viewer that Tillis's portrayal of the Queen of Denial is full of irony. At the very end of the video, she winks at the camera and at the viewer. "Cleopatra, Queen of Denial," like the humorous music videos discussed in chapter 2, shows the ways in which humor can be used to expose the sexism in romantic conventions. What is most compelling about "Cleopatra, Queen of Denial" is that, unlike "The Home-coming Queen's Got a Gun," for example, Tillis ridicules a thematic mainstay of her own genre. In this regard, her music video is representative of dozens of feminist country music videos. In 1994 Pam Tillis's achievements were recognized when she was named Female Vocalist of the Year, due in part to her hit "Cleopatra, Queen of Denial."

Humor appears frequently in music videos by feminist country music performers; another example is Tanya Tucker's "Hangin' In," in which the mournful tune and lyrics describe a woman pining away for her loved man, while the video images reveal an unrepentant Tucker cavorting at the beach. Reba McEntire, Dolly Parton and others use humor to contravene romantic conventions. In this vein, Tillis's "Cleopatra, Queen of Denial" draws on the pun, featured on T-shirts, but turns to a wry commentary on the country tradition of "cheatin'" (Rogers 126–62). Humor is here used to implement a role reversal and commentary on gender roles, especially the position of woman as victim of love in country music songs.

While Tillis and other female performers rely primarily on humor to create a feminist message, some performers use a little humor in combination with other strategies, such as a postmodern style. Suzy Bogguss also criticizes romantic narratives, but more directly than Tillis does. Like Julie Brown, Bogguss was herself a homecoming queen and a cheerleader (Kosser 212). In 1988, Bogguss won the Academy of Country Music's Best New Country Female Vocalist Award.

In Bogguss's "Hey Cinderella" the singer turns to another feminine fantasy—this time the fairy tale story of Cinderella, rescued from the ashes by Prince Charming. Bogguss here situates herself as part of a feminist tradition exposing the perfidiousness of fairy tales for women (see Gilbert and Gubar 1987; Zipes). She also uses humor—a more subtle irony in both lyrics and images—to critique this trap for women. Bogguss imagines the character of Cinderella as a fellow sister, whom she addresses: "Hey Cinderella, what's the story all about? I've got a funny feeling we missed a page or two." Bogguss depicts a marriage in which there is no happy ending as in the fairy tale. Even though we outgrow the toys of childhood, the power of the fairy tale romance lingers: "Dolls gather dust in the corner of the attic, and bicycles rust in the rain. / But still we walk in that fabled shadow and sometimes we call her name / Hey Cinderella." The discrepancy between real life and fiction causes the singer to ask Cinderella, "Does the shoe fit you now?" That Cinderella's shoe doesn't fit is rendered visually when a plastic shoe falls off a young girl's foot and floats away in the ocean. Young girls don't fit such shoes, but are encouraged by fairy tales to grow into them.

As is standard in women's country music videos, there are a number of close-ups of Bogguss's face as she lip-synchs the lyrics. This aspect of the video makes it seem as though Bogguss herself is addressing the viewer directly; such an intimate shot exudes sincerity and is a video extension of the "sincerity contract." Bogguss cowrote the song, as every viewer can tell from the credits, so the direct address is even more persuasive: she is singing her own words. These close-ups of Bogguss are cut with depictions of three other female figures: a young girl, an elderly woman and a young bride. The montage suggests the fragmentation of the female self. In the first shots, a young girl is playing in the ocean; a tiered wedding cake is on the shore. In a number of different sequences, the girl runs over to the wedding cake, first with a Ken doll in her hand and then with a wedding bouquet. She seems fascinated by these items— social conditioning depicted via visual shorthand. An older woman dressed as a fairy godmother, complete with wand, stands in the background. In between, we see shots of a bride and groom in a fairy tale castle, happy at first, and then increasingly alienated and separated. Another feature of the tale, a pumpkin, appears in the girl's hand, then on the bridegroom's head; finally, the bride throws the pumpkin over the castle wall. The music video ends as the fairy godmother destroys the wedding cake, and then cavorts off into the ocean by herself. The air of fantasy is enhanced by the addition of an unreal purple to the sky. As do the lyrics, the images debunk the fairy tale notion of romance, revealing that the story is only a fiction and an unhealthy one at that. It is the fairy tale that entices the young happy girl into being the unhappy wife, but there is hope, for the older woman is able to demolish the wedding myth and stride off through the water, as happy as the young girl was at the beginning of the video. In its close-ups of the older woman, of Bogguss, and of the young girl, this music video represents a radical change from most music videos: "Hey Cinderella" represents a range of femininity, not just the sexually desirable young woman.

Bogguss's video differs from most country music videos in its clever and innovative use of the postmodern form.[6] The visual images are marked by jump cuts, fragmentation, the alternation of black and white with color images, and the surreal addition of color to both the sky and the sea. The linear narration that is part of most country music videos is radically disrupted. The use of postmodern qualities discussed in chapter 1 is even more effective than in, for example, Annie Lennox's "Why," because it disrupts the televisual flow more radically on TNN or CMT than Lennox does on MTV, where many videos employ a postmodern visual style. The bizarre juxtapositions reconfigure the fairy tale plot of "Cinderella": the pumpkin is no longer the coach but instead sits on the groom's head, making him look ridiculous, and then appears as a jack-o'-lantern over the young girl's head, suggesting how the story deforms her visions of herself and her future. That the bride is played by either Bogguss herself or someone who looks like her repeats the idea of Everywoman present in Julie Brown's video, "The Homecoming Queen's Got a Gun," in which Brown plays both the Homecoming Queen and her best friend who comments on the events. Bogguss can comment on the fairy tale while also being caught up in it. The surreal colors visually stress that the fairy tale is, as the lyrics explain, unreal and unworkable as a life script.

Other country music videos that similarly criticize fairy tale ideas of romance as unworkable for women are Mary-Chapin Carpenter's "He Thinks He'll Keep Her," discussed at the end of this chapter, "Tears Dry," performed by Victoria Shaw, "Now I Know," performed by Lari White, "Break These Chains," by Deborah Allen, and "You Hurt Me Bad in a Real Good Way," performed by Patty Loveless. All these music videos undercut the romantic ideal of a forever and perfect love.

While some feminist performers expose the sexism of fairy tale romance, others take a straightforward and direct approach to women's issues. Country music videos illustrating extreme cases of oppression—for example, sexual harassment and domestic violence—include the same features found in other feminist music videos, such as direct address, but exclude the attempt to entertain. Linda Davis's "Company Time," for example, addresses sexual harassment. An even more disturbing and effective music video, Martina McBride's compelling "Independence Day," depicts the effects of domestic violence on the battered woman's daughter. (This video won the 1994 Country Music Award for Music Video of the Year.) Written by Gretchen Peters, the song lyrics tell a daughter's story of her mother's fight back against an abusive husband. The young girl is featured prominently, as is the young girl in "Hey Cinderella." Also as in Bogguss's video, there are numerous close-ups of the singer, adding a touch of veracity, intensity and intimacy as she recounts the disastrous events of an Independence Day when the narrator was eight. The lyrics and images are a resounding condemnation of domestic violence.

With apocalyptic language, the lyrics evoke the notion of independence and resistance: "Let freedom ring / Let the white dove sing / Let the whole world know that today is the day of reckoning." A clear parallel is drawn between the notion of national independence and the right of a woman to be free from domestic tyranny and enslavement. The refrain continues to stress role reversal, again in apocalyptic terms: "Let the weak be strong / Let the right be wrong / Roll the stone away / Let the guilty pay / It's Independence Day." The aura of judgment day is strong and compelling. The lyrics clearly condemn the community for allowing domestic violence and for failing to aid the battered wife. "Some folks talked and some folks listened, but everybody looked the other way / And when time ran out there was no one about."

The visual images strengthen and underline the brutality of domestic violence and encourage the viewer to identify and sympathize with the abused mother, who finally, in desperation, burns down her house and presumably herself and her husband. The video opens with an overhead shot of the mother affectionately touching her daughter's hair as they both sing "Amazing Grace." This incorporation of a section from another song is an illustration of postmodern "sampling," common in rap music. Referring to another musical tradition, the video comments on religious faith and its inefficacy in a situation of domestic violence. This endearing portrait of mother-daughter affection is disrupted by shots of the mother crying and of the father, shown only from the neck down, angrily striding through the house. The mother's tear-stained face is shown, a bruise prominently displayed, and her hands tremble as she covers her face. The scenes of domestic threats and violence are cut with scenes from the Independence Day parade from downtown and shots of McBride singing on Main Street, with a flag behind her. The scenes of violence are all the more disturbing because of this juxtaposition with scenes of parade frivolity and celebration. The unhappy daughter and abused wife are contrasted with the ebullient flag girls and drum major. The drum major is commanding the band, while the wife and daughter cannot even command their own movements. The town's complicity in condoning domestic violence is vividly depicted as two clowns, one male and one female, spar with each other to the delight of the crowd. The scene is made stronger because it is shot from below, as though we are seeing the clowns fight and the crowd's delight from the young girl's diminutive perspective. The daughter stares horrified at this depiction of violence and the crowd's reaction, and then runs for home. Meanwhile, we see her father throw the mother across the room and to the floor; he appears to choke her, and then he sweeps everything off a mantel, sending delicate pottery crashing against the wall. As the abused wife sits alone on the floor, she lights a match and drops it. By the time the daughter returns to their house, it is aflame.

The conflagration is reminiscent of another television depiction of domestic violence, "The Burning Bed." In the music video, however, the flames again evoke the notion of apocalypse and destruction. The house and the family are destroyed from within. As the daughter desperately cries "Momma," a fireman and then the police carry her away. We see her tear-stained face. The filming of all these scenes in black and white reinforces the sense of flashback and documentary licensed by the phrasing of the lyrics. The "sincerity contract" is upheld by the vividness and verisimilitude of these images. This sense of immediacy is underscored by McBride's impassioned singing of the song and her direct address to the camera. She claims, "Now I ain't saying if it's right or wrong, but maybe it's the only way"; even this equivocation is contradicted by the visual narrative, which depicts the pain and desperation of battering, and in so doing explains and justifies the battered woman's actions. The close-ups of McBride first feature the burning house, and then Main Street, juxtaposing the destruction of the domicile to the emptiness of Main Street framed by the red, white and blue bunting that celebrates national independence but provides neither security nor independence for wife or daughter. McBride draws upon what Fenster describes as one of the conventions of country music videos—the depiction of small-town life. But here small-town life is exposed as dangerous for women. In the final frames, McBride is dwarfed by an enormous American flag hanging to her right. She looks away, forcing us to see the small figure of a woman and an immense but empty symbol of our national independence. "Independence Day" is perhaps the strongest and most direct feminist country music video discussed here, but it exists in a continuum of feminist messages that makes its brutal directness less shocking.

Martina McBride, Pam Tillis and Suzy Bogguss were three of over sixty participants in "The Women of Country," a CBS prime-time special, which aired in 1992. Like "Sisters in the Name of Rap," a pay-for-view special that presented dozens of female rappers, and which is discussed in the next chapter, "The Women of Country," by its very existence, demonstrates the importance and popularity of the genre's female performers. The special also demonstrates the mainstreaming of country music. Its appearance on a network, rather than on one of the specialized country music channels, shows how widespread and popular the genre has become. Its performers are no longer presumed to speak only for southerners, for a rural population, or for the working class. At the same time, the exclusive focus on women performers shows that they have a proven appeal and legitimacy as women. The number of women performers who appear is in itself impressive, and so is their range. From the genre's early foremothers like Rose Maddox and Patsy Montana to the stars of its middle years like Loretta Lynn and Tammy Wynette and finally to the stars from the 1980s and 1990s like Pam Tillis, Patty Loveless and Mary-Chapin Carpenter, the female performers are all articulate. The existence of the show not only marks the importance and prominence of individual female performers but also indicates an acceptance and an interest in them as women.

The format consists of segments covering the history of women in country music. Archival photographs and old film clips depict the images of women in country music, from sweetheart singer to cowboy gal to new country. There are twelve performances, beginning and ending with group numbers. Interspersed between the snippets of history and performances are interviews with the singers themselves, addressing primarily the roles and restrictions faced by female performers. Throughout the special, we are shown scenes of rehearsal and backstage intimacy. These sequences are paralleled by a number of shots of a highly appreciative audience in a huge auditorium as the female country music stars perform. The emphasis on audience corroborates the notion that country music performers have a special and close relationship with their fans. The stars themselves claim, as Susan Longacre explains on the program, that "the audience is largely female and they [record companies] realize women can speak for other women"; this special verifies that the fans are primarily women. The music video that was culled from the program, "He Thinks He'll Keep Her," performed by Mary-Chapin Carpenter, with choral support from Suzy Bogguss, Kathy Mattea, Trisha Yearwood, Emmylou Harris, Patty Loveless, and Pam Tillis, alternates between shots of the women singing together and their female fans. A few shots of the male stage band only accentuate the commonalities between the singers and their fans.

Notions of sisterhood and feminism are also made quite explicit through the interviews with the performers. Their words reinforce the sense of solidarity and sisterhood depicted in the visual images of the collaborative performances and the shots of rehearsals and of affectionate greetings. Several of the younger performers pay tribute to their country music foremothers. Lorrie Morgan, for example, acknowledges that "the reason that it's happening for us today is because of our idols, people like Tammy Wynette, Loretta Lynn, Patsy Cline." Kathy Mattea similarly stresses the debts that today's generation of female performers owes to its predecessors: "If these women hadn't been out there, as the only woman in a gang of men, paving the way for us, that especially makes me feel part of a heritage." Pam Tillis asserts that "women who pioneered country music *are* country music." More humorously, but undoubtedly just as sincerely, she adds, "I just hope I'm worthy to walk a mile in their high heels."

Feminist ideals are raised both implicitly and explicitly by the performers, songwriters, and producers. A number of the women verbalize their appreciation of female solidarity in country music. Jeanne Seely says, "You know when you have the same dreams and goal and face the same problems, there has to be a sisterhood." Martina McBride praises the help she received as a newcomer from other women, and Sylvia pays tribute to the experience of the special itself: "It was really wonderful, a wonderful experience to be in a room with all these other *women* entertainers. It was just a real affirming experience." Sylvia's enthusiasm is corroborated by the viewer as well as by her fellow performers. Recognition of feminist values in combination with denial of an overly strong identification with feminism seems to be a common stance among women country music performers. Trisha Yearwood, for example, explains, "I'm not this card-carrying feminist. I believe in being feminine and being a woman and all that, but it's OK to do that and also to be strong and not be stepped on" (Kingsbury 1992a, 18). While Michelle Wright feels compelled to introduce one of her songs by explaining, "This song is not a man-bashing song; it's just a guideline for all you fellows out there," the feminist message of "The Women of Country Music" is unequivocal. As Lacy J. Dalton explains, "Unless we really make a fuss, nobody's going to listen to us." The Forester Sisters, whose infamous song "Men" is a litany of complaints about sexism, respond to the loaded query "Are you card-carrying feminists?" by

saying clearly, "Well, actions speak louder than words."
And Susan Dunn explains her position thus: "The women
in my songs are fairly strong . . . they get hurt and they
retaliate." It is the feminist message in the songs, however, that makes the point about actions clear. The performances contain strong, compelling messages about
women's subordination, and the performances themselves provide resistance to women's oppression.

The opening number, a popular song by Mary-Chapin
Carpenter entitled "He Thinks He'll Keep Her," is about
a woman leaving her husband. That Carpenter opens
and closes the special surely signifies the changes made
by women in country music. She is described as "bring-
ing a particularly modern female sensibility to country.
She writes about characters who are self-sufficient and
independent, who shape their own lives rather than allowing themselves to be defined by their men" (Schoemer 37). This song is a good example of Carpenter's
writing, but is also representative of feminist country
music, as the videos previously discussed and the other
performances in the special demonstrate. The refrain
"He thinks he'll keep her," an ironic reference to the
husband's taking his wife for granted and to a notorious
commercial for Geritol, is compelling especially when
it rises from the voices of the chorus of six famous
and influential performers. The lyrics comment on the
unpaid and unappreciated work of a homemaker: "For
fifteen years she had a job and not one raise in pay."
Through the lyrics and by implication, the performers
support the wife's decision to leave her husband, but the
words also comment on the adversity that she faces in
a hostile and sexist job market: "Now she's in the typing
pool on minimum wage." The camera shows Carpenter

shaking her head as she sings these words, emphasizing her disapproval.

Both Suzy Bogguss and Trisha Yearwood sing songs about the importance of friendship, songs that, in the context of this special, seem particularly to be about women's relationships with each other. Pam Tillis sings her crowd-pleaser "Cleopatra, Queen of Denial," discussed earlier, with Suzy Bogguss, Mary-Chapin Carpenter, and Emmylou Harris as her back-up singers. The humor in "Cleopatra, Queen of Denial" is picked up when Tanya Tucker does a sly Elvis imitation in "It's a Little Too Late," a clever song about how it is too late to do the right thing now. Attired in a honky-tonk bright red dress with a petticoat, Tucker asserts the right of women to be "bad," too. The color red and women's sexual desires are elaborated on by Lorrie Morgan, whose "Something in Red" chronicles the stages in a woman's life through the colors of her clothes: red for dating, white for marriage, blue after her child is born, and then red again as she struggles to reassert her sexuality. Tammy Wynette even does a victim number, but one that asserts the singer's pride and self-respect, for she'll do her crying in the rain, so that her former lover won't have the satisfaction of seeing her distraught. Patty Loveless develops this idea of the strong sufferer in her triumphant song "You Hurt Me Bad in a Real Good Way." In the lyrics, she describes her discovery of love after a break-up—the notion of a fortunate fall.

The show-stopping number, however, is "Everything We Got We Got the Hard Way." The number begins with Mary-Chapin Carpenter, who is joined at first by one and then two other performers, until finally the stage is flooded with almost all the women we have seen interviewed during the show, singing in unison. The lyrics ask, "Show a little inspiration / Show a little spark," which these performers most certainly do. They sing together of the difficulties faced by female performers, a theme of many of the interviews, but they also sing triumphantly, "We got this far by never turning back." They claim the power to work and sing, "We've got two lives, the one we're given and the one we make." In an allusion to the vexing issue of whether to call themselves feminists, they sing, "The world won't stop, actions speak louder." In a final repudiation of love when it traps and confines women, the refrain changes to "We got this far not by love, but by never turning back." The camera angles throughout stress the variety and the range of female country music performers, as well as their connection to the audience. The camera looks from behind the vast crowd, then zooms in on the performers, then back to the crowd again. As the credits for the program roll, we see the women having a group portrait taken. It is a fitting conclusion to an inspiring special and a moment that reminds viewers again of the solidarity of this group of women. The television special reveals that it is a new day for country music and for the women performers as well. By celebrating their female solidarity, they reach a segment of the population that has been neglected by feminists.

These examples of feminist country music videos demonstrate that feminist messages are wide-ranging and have reached genres that many academic feminists may be unaware of. The success of feminist country music performers suggests that their feminist messages are reaching a receptive audience. In country music more than in other mass music genres, the performer's identity and image are closely linked with the message. As Fenster points out, country music videos are a way to reach audiences who would otherwise not listen to country music (112), but feminist performers do more than promote the genre. In their music videos, although these female performers are promoting themselves and marketing their music, they are at the same time selling to the huge country audience the message that women's subordination is unacceptable and that strong, powerful female voices can and will be heard.

Chapter Six

"Sisters in the Name of Rap": Feminist Rap Music Videos

U. N. I. T. Y. . . . a Black woman from infinity to
infinity   —Queen Latifah

Although they have been featured in a number of newspaper articles, feminist rappers have not
received sufficient critical attention. Three recent books
on rap (Spencer; Costello and Wallace; Toop) ignore
female rappers, and, as recently as March 1990, Terry
Teachout could proclaim that "not surprisingly, women
in the world of rap are largely, if not exclusively, objects
of transient sexual gratification" (60). Feminist rappers
like Queen Latifah, Yo-Yo, Ms. Melodie, Salt 'n Pepa, M. C.
Lyte, and Roxanne, among others, belie his pronouncement. Feminist rappers especially deserve close attention
because they are a group of African-American women
who are "allowed to speak their own words," a situation
that Michelle Wallace identifies as unusual in popular
culture (1990a, 3). One of two exceptions to the critical
neglect of feminist rappers is Tricia Rose, whose article
"Never Trust a Big Butt and a Smile," similarly calls for
"broadening the scope of investigations in our search
for black women's voices" (128) to include rap (see also
Keyes). Rose asserts that "women rappers are vocal and
respected members of the Hip Hop community, and they
have quite a handle on what they're doing (109). Female

rappers have been actively involved in social issues such as abortion and birth control.[1]

In her book on rap, *Black Noise: Rap Music and Black Culture in Contemporary America*, Rose devotes a chapter to female rappers. She describes women rappers as "integral and resistant voices in rap music . . . who sustain an ongoing dialogue with their audiences and with male rappers" (146). She emphasizes that female rappers have been misinterpreted as being in opposition to male rappers, when the actual situation is more complicated than one of feminist rappers versus misogynist rappers. For example, she cites the refusal of many prominent female rappers (including Salt 'n Pepa and Queen Latifah) to criticize 2 Live Crew's use of female bodies, explaining that the female rappers realized that they would just be used by the media in a racist way that would not help African-American women (148–49).

This chapter and the following one build on Rose's understanding of female rappers, but place them in the context of postmodernism and of other women music video performers. While Rose discusses a few music videos, these two chapters discuss in great detail what Rose describes: female rappers' "visual presence in music videos and live performances display[ing] exuberant communities of women occupying public space, sexual freedom, independence and occasionally explicit domination over men" (170). Significantly, once again a site of this expression is a television special, this time devoted to female rappers rather than to women in country music.

Like country music women, female rappers are reluctant about or refuse altogether the label "feminist." Also like women in the country music genre, female rappers have benefited from an increased interest in women performers. As Rose explains, "For a number of reasons, including increased record industry support and more demand for rappers generally and female rappers specifically, women have greater access to production and transportation resources" (154).

Rap, or hip hop, as "the culture of clothes, slang, dances, and philosophies that sprang up in the '80s" (George 40) is sometimes called, was seen daily on the special MTV program *Yo MTV Raps* and on *Rap City*, an hour-long show on BET. While *Yo MTV Raps* still exists in a weekly format, rap music videos have made the shift to the general playlist, and they appear especially on *MTV Jams*, a two-hour segment aired twice daily. These shows frequently air music videos by female performers, and many rap videos, like "Push It" and "Shoop" by Salt 'n Pepa, the first female rap group to go platinum, and "Supersonic" by J. J. Fad, received heavy rotation outside the rap shows. Rap's increasing popularity has been accompanied by the appearance of a number of feminist performers, including (The Real) Roxanne, M. C. Lyte, Shelly Thunder, Roxanne Shante, J. J. Fad, Salt 'n Pepa, Queen Latifah, Sweet Tee, Ms. Melodie, Antoinette, and Precious and by crossovers like Paula Abdul and Neneh Cherry. These performers draw on rap specifically as an African-American art form to resist racism; yet unlike most of their fellow male rappers, feminist rappers draw additional energy from their simultaneous discussion of race and gender. Evoking the specters of racism and sexism enables them to attack these issues more effectively, because, unlike other political videos, feminist rap videos point to the ways in which systems of oppression are linked and are interdependent. Their message is particularly powerful in the context of the other videos that air on MTV and BET. In this frame, the feminist rap videos are always, already, radical.

Rap, like all other forms of popular music, is not inherently feminist or political, and indeed some well-known rap songs like Tone Loc's "Wild Thing" are obnoxiously sexist. However, female performers manage in this genre, as in other popular genres, to use specific generic qualities to promote a feminist message.

Rap is noted for its strong rhythm, often only a percussive beat, and its emphasis on lyrics. The melody in a rap song frequently follows the performer's enunciation of lyrics, which usually rhyme and involve clever linguistic plays on meaning and sound. Through the lyrics, female rappers make explicit and overt assertions of female strength and autonomy. The focus of the group is the rap performer rather than instrumentalists or record scratchers (the "disc jockeys" who manipulate records to produce that sound unique to rap of a record being moved back and forth rapidly). In rap, particular stress is laid upon the performer's personality and name. As described by a participant in street rap, rap is "about competition and gaining attention . . . 'Listen to my story, about myself, life and romance; and listen while I tell it to the beat of the music. There's poetry here, and I'll tell you anything without missing a beat'" (Ewen 56). While this description was produced by a male rapper, it applies equally well to female rappers. Since rap revolves around self-promotion, female rappers are able to use the form without being accused of being self-centered or narcissistic.

The dynamic of rap requires that the performer focus on personal narrative, which, in the hands of a female rapper, can produce a feminist tale. As Cheryl L.

Keyes writes, "In general, women express through the rap medium their personal feelings about female and male relationships, but more important, they speak for the empowerment of women" (216). Female rappers compete with male performers and gain attention for their feminist message through music videos, which also, as Simon Frith argues, function to draw attention to the performer. He writes, "Whether as video-art or as video-promotion, clips work as self-portraits: they represent their performers to their fans" (216). Cornel West identifies this quality of self-promotion as distinctively African-American: "A distinctive feature of these black styles is a certain projection of self—more a persona—in performance. This is not simply a self-investment and self-involvement in musical, rhetorical, and athletic enactments; it also acknowledges radical contingency and even solicits challenge and danger" (West 93). The challenge and danger that he describes is redoubled in feminist rap because of the paradoxically strong position black female performers have as a result of their perspective, being both a part of the rap scene and opposing its misogyny.

Rap has been described by Jon Pareles as "music shaped by the most pervasive instrument of American popular culture—commercial television," but rappers, especially female rappers, are, he says, "turning television's rhythms to their own ends" (1). Through music videos, female performers can use the televisual mechanisms to promote and strengthen their feminist messages. Using clothes, camera address, dance, and visual images, female rappers enhance their depictions of female power and representations of female sexual desire.

Significantly, rap contains postmodernist qualities, an aspect of the music that has been ignored, perhaps because it is usually associated with white, "high," masculine culture. I agree with West, who says, "For too long, the postmodernism debate has remained inscribed within narrow disciplinary boundaries, insulated artistic practices, and vague formulations of men and women of letters" (90). Rap music videos provide a site for the exploration of postmodernism in the intersection of African-American and mass culture. "Scratching" demonstrates a postmodern quality of rap because it involves the appropriation of another record. This method of producing music and the frequent use of snatches of melody from other songs as part of a rap record—"dubbing" or "sampling"—emphasize pastiche and fragmentation, two fundamental aspects of postmodernism. Drawing on diverse styles is an essential part of postmodernism. While scratching is postmodern when it appears in conjunction with music videos' other postmodern qualities, such as fragmentation, pastiche, and self-reflexivity, it is also an adaptation of African-American or Afro-Caribbean "versioning." As described by Hebdige, versioning is "an invocation of someone else's voice to help you say what you want to say" (14). Hebdige positions this characteristic as explicitly African-American and Afro-Caribbean, complaining that this quality "is often cited by critics in a spirit of censure" (14). Like Angela Davis and David Toop, Hebdige connects adaptation and emphasis on rhythm to the use of music by African slaves to "express their resentment, anger and frustration" (26). Rap music videos demonstrate another feature of postmodernism—that of grafting older forms of art onto newer manifestations.

Rap music videos belong to a long and venerable tradition of rapping in African-American culture, including, for example, the tradition of the toast (see Keyes; Saloy). Rap itself draws on qualities of non-Western music that overlap with postmodernism.

Feminist rappers draw not only on postmodernism and Afrocentrism but also on the female-centered tradition of blues queens. The similarity of blues to rap is stressed by one of the most prominent of feminist rappers, Queen Latifah: "We can go way back to the roaring '20s, to black women blues singers. Blues is rap, just singing it" (Rose 1990, 16). While female blues singers did focus on melancholia, Daphne Duval Harrison argues that blues songs like "Every Dog Has His Day," performed by Sippie Wallace, involve "an assertion of power" (89). Harrison explains that "women began to use the blues as a positive means of retaliation" (89) and argues that women's blues in the 1920s "represented a distinctly female interpretation. The choice of performing style, inflection, emphasis and improvisation on certain aspects of lyrics gave a perspective and expressiveness that had a profound effect . . . [these singers] introduced a new, different model of black women—more assertive, sexy, sexually aware, independent, realistic, complex, alive" (111). Yet for the feminist rapper, rap offers unique possibilities. What Barbara Christian suggests about blues singers applies here to the more optimistic musical form, rap: "Perhaps because the blues was seen as 'race music' and catered to a black audience, black women were better able to articulate themselves as individuals and as part of a racial group in that art form" (122).

To use Nelson George's words, rap is "cartoony, antimelodic, brooding, materialistic, entrepreneurial, chauvinistic, user-friendly, genital conscious, and always spoiling for a fight" (40). West's description of general African-American cultural practices also accurately depicts rap: "By kinetic orality, I mean dynamic repetitive and energetic rhetorical styles that form communities, e.g., antiphonal styles and linguistic innovations that accent fluid, improvisational identities and that promote survival at almost any cost. By passionate physicality, I mean bodily stylizations of the world, syncopations, and polyrhythms that assert one's somebodiness in a society in which one's body has no public worth, only economic value as a laboring metabolism" (93). These are the qualities of rap that feminist performers draw on.

In M. C. Lyte's "Lyte as a Rock," the song title and refrain, with its clever play on sound and language, is a means of self-promotion. Lyte uses the characteristics of rap to emphasize her feminist self-assertion. She plays with the sound of her name and with the notion of metaphor and simile to emphasize her own importance. "I am the Lyte" is one refrain that stresses her reinterpretation of history, her illuminating perspective. It recalls, of course, descriptions of Christ as the light, suggesting how radical, even heretical, Lyte's revisioning is. Debating in the rap whether "Lyte as a rock" is a metaphor or a simile shows that she even dominates English class. "LYTE STRIKES AGAIN" reads the headline of the newspaper that appears in both the scene with gangsters and the one in the prison cell. In both instances, the idea of lightning striking evokes the suggestion of power that Lyte is claiming for herself. Unfortunately, in two of the instances, Lyte pushes out another woman and replaces her as a figure of power. But the overall criticism of symbolic structures of language and history is marred rather than destroyed by these moments.

Lyte's video uses a postmodern style to address issues of history and education in an intense and moving fashion. The video opens with an allusion to the tremendously popular *Star Wars*, a film that similarly opened with an introduction blazing across the backdrop of stars. These credits tell us that M. C. Lyte is "Lyte as a Rock." With this opening, Lyte asserts her ambitions for this video and identifies herself as a feisty fighter like the heroes of the extremely popular science fiction movie. These opening frames also set the video up as a fairy tale, for, like *Star Wars*, this video is a fable, directed toward a young girl shown picking up a doll and opening a door.

The door frames images of Lyte throughout history, beginning in prehistoric times. This survey constantly reminds the viewers of a variety of oppressions, from the identification of cavemen as symbols of male dominance through Egyptian slave society and the oppressiveness of gangster violence (a response here to gangsta rap and its acceptance of violence against women) to the separatist resistance evoked by the picture of Malcolm X when Lyte is in a prison cell. The jail operates as a sign of racial oppression, but is appropriated here also to be a reference to the oppression of women. Salt 'n Pepa and many other women rappers depict a scene in a jail to make just this point (Rose 1994, 167).

Lyte's video gives snapshots of history from a female perspective, with a number of interruptions as Lyte the rapper comments and involves herself in the scenes. First we watch a young girl journey through a cave, in a scene reminiscent of Lyte's own development. Lyte explains, "I'm a rapper who is here to make things the way they ought to be," declaring, "I can't be stopped, I am Lyte as a rock." Observing a series of historical settings in the video, Lyte first watches another woman shield her child from a caveman and interjects with her strong, assertive message: "Move out of the way." She continues through history, confronting other strong women in Egyptian times and then in a gangster setting. She finally appears in a jail cell and locks the door with a key. Here the camera pans a poster of Malcolm X, suggesting the black rights movement as a lineage from which Lyte draws strength. The setting dissolves into a classroom where her backup explains that "Lyte as a rock" is a simile. This reference to simile stresses that history and education are systems, which Lyte herself resists and literally dissolves when her image takes over the blackboard. How alien traditional history and education are to black women is emphasized when Lyte is described as being from "the planet of Brooklyn." She begins smiling and dancing. Finally the young girl waves good-bye and closes the door on a panorama of stars.

This survey of history seems designed to criticize history and education for the young girl's edification. As Lyte explains, "By the tone of my voice you can tell I'm a scholar"—an identification supported by the video's images of history and the appearance of Lyte's words in a classroom. Her feminist revision of history is emphasized through her plays on language, which point to her correction of these events. Her preaching—"This is the way it is, don't ever forget"—refers both to her reinterpretation of history and to her own stance of strength. In the Egyptian frames, Lyte lectures the lighter-colored woman she has ejected from the bier, taking over the position of ruler and directing her words to the young girl, who seems delighted. "I show stability, potential and strength," Lyte declares, so forcefully that the viewer is inclined to take her at her word. It's believable when she explains that "Lyte is here, no one can stop me." She goes on, "Never underestimate Lyte DMC, I am the rapper here to make things the way they're meant to be." "Meant to be" means less racist and sexist, especially in the context of the video's images. Lyte identifies herself with women through the doubled image of herself as Cleopatra and in present-day dress as well as through the implication that the young girl is or could become like herself. With her reference to Cleopatra, Lyte also connects with an image repeated throughout feminist music videos, most notably Pam Tillis's "Cleopatra, Queen of Denial." She then declares, "Guys watch me even some girls clock me." Like other feminist rappers, she declares her right to sexual desire. Using images of herself as a seductive and powerful Cleopatra and then as the leader of a gang in the 1940s, Lyte adapts these allusions to project female power. The image of Lyte from the 1940s directly connects her to blues singers, an association strengthened when Lyte refers to another black singer, Grace Jones. When Lyte declares she is a "slave to the rhythm," she is alluding to a song of the same name by Jones, an important and influential contemporary performer. Like Jones's use of the phrase, Lyte's choice of the word "slave" recalls a specific moment in the history of racism: literal enslavement.

Lyte uses a postmodern sensibility to make her feminist critique of racism and sexism. Postmodern references are apparent in the style of the video, particularly in the use of the door, of her giant face in contrast to the little girl's image, and in the revision of history implicit in the costume and setting changes. Postmodern influence also appears in the doubling of Lyte as both Cleopatra and her contemporary self and in the blackboard that dissolves into a video image of Lyte's face. Lyte demonstrates a keen sense of her lineage and of history in the allusions to Jones and slavery and in the poster of Malcolm X that appears in the jail cell. In this scene, as in Salt 'n Pepa's video, which is discussed next, jail functions as a reminder both of how black men are imprisoned by white patriarchal culture and of how black women can similarly be trapped by sexism. Lyte turns this image around, for she has the key to the cell and explains that she is not trapped, but that others are. The video's frame of a young girl dangling her doll and staring entranced at Lyte's image emphasizes the positive and formative aspects of videos like this one. The young girl might be Lyte herself, dreaming of her future, or she might be Lyte's audience. Either way, Lyte demonstrates that postmodern style and rap style can work together to make a feminist statement about strong women. Her video reinterprets history from an African-American woman's perspective, and her revisioning is depicted as being educational at the same time that it is entertaining.

Salt 'n Pepa have been explicit about their feminist purpose: in an interview on MTV, they described their music as depicting "a female point of view. I guess you could call what we do feminist. We believe in standing up for your rights." Their videos consistently assert the rights of women to control their own bodies and to proclaim their desires. As their name suggests, the two work together; their partnership itself points to a feminist cooperation. The extent of their partnership is reflected in the dialogue structure of their rapping. One of them begins a line, the other finishes it and then they speak simultaneously. With a wry sense of humor and witty play with language, their first and second videos, "Push It" and "Shake Your Thang," demonstrate their feminist convictions. Throughout, Salt 'n Pepa appropriate the use of masculine language to reclaim sexuality and to assert their right to speak of desire. Their images and language contest phallic sexuality whether they are "standing up" for their rights and/or discussing men. As Salt said in *People* magazine, "We're feminists. . . . We're doing something that only guys are expected to do and doin' it RIGHT!" (Gaar 424).

As "Shake Your Thang" opens, they are being arrested for "dirty dancing" and harangued by a group of men, presumably police detectives. The implications in terms of racism and sexism are clear. The images of arrest, imprisonment, protests and release recall the unjust incarceration of civil rights leaders. In reference to the similarity between racism and sexism, the jailers are all male. The two do not take their arrest quietly. They both complain, and Pepa grabs a detective by the tie, shouting twice at him an action the phallic significance of which is obvious. Pepa takes patriarchy by the phallus. The scene then switches to a group of women dancing together, greatly relishing their own performance. They are being addressed by a male who urges them on, using words from the Isley Brothers's 1969 hit "It's Your Thing": "It's your thing—do what you want to do—I can't tell you who to sock it to." This masculine support for their music and dancing is only the beginning, for Pepa takes over the lyrics and proclaims, "It's my thing." They may accept inspiration and support from a male leader, but they quickly move to make the declaration of independence their own. Part of their "thing"—their independence—involves dancing together, eschewing men. At the end of the video, one of the men informs the leader that "we gotta let them go, captain" and the two women march off triumphantly. The reflection of the bars suggests that the men are imprisoned, a parallel to Lyte's explanation that others are imprisoned, not she. This conclusion emphasizes the optimism and energy of the feminist rap video, in which the female rappers are always vindicated.

This video contains several elements typical of the feminist rap video. First, Salt 'n Pepa assert their right to express sexual desire and to control their own bodies. This is a central part of feminism, especially in the context of music videos, in which women are most frequently used as objects of desire for a male gaze. Their resistance becomes apparent in the first frames when their mug shots are being taken. Each woman smiles rebelliously and seductively, both acknowledging the camera and controlling it self-consciously. This moment should be read as the key to the rest of the video and a sign of the postmodern, self-reflexive nature of video. In this postmodern moment, Salt 'n Pepa both acknowledge and refute exploitative use of the female body, a position that places them in the same arena with radical feminists like Ellen Willis, who argues that women have a right to express sexual desire without caving in to the male gaze. Salt 'n Pepa make this point when they declare, "It's my dance / It's my body."

Second, the corollary to control of their own bodies is a refusal to allow men to presume that control. Salt 'n Pepa announce, "If a guy touches my body I put him in check / I say you can't do that we just met." In a response undoubtedly aimed at male rappers like Young M. C. and Afrika Bambatta, who repeatedly accuse women of being rapacious golddiggers, they declare, "We don't want your money." Similarly, Salt 'n Pepa are shown triumphing over a group of men—the police—who would restrict them. As we have seen, a jail scene is common in feminist rap videos as a representation of female incarceration through sexism. In line with the self-promotional aspects of the video, the female artists invariably succeed in circumventing male authority. As Pepa said in the MTV interview: "Especially do something somebody tell you not to do." This is the same point she makes in the video when she grabs the police captain's tie and declares: "We're going to do what we want to do." Even the incorporation of the older song "It's Your Thing" into their video ends up being an appropriation, for Salt 'n Pepa rework the 1969 song into a feminist rap. The idea of movements building upon other movements, as this rap song builds on the 1960s classic, shows how this particular attribute of rap works to intensify the feminist message of the video. Through this dynamic, Salt 'n Pepa suggest that the use of race and gender as a positive collaboration can supply a model for ways to resist oppression. In fact, they go further and suggest that black men should not and cannot imprison black women.

As they make this case, however, there is an unpleasant moment when Pepa accuses the police captain of being "fruity."[2] This homophobia reveals that not even a feminist rap music video, any more than the rest of popular culture, can escape the taint of prejudice. In drawing attention to Salt 'n Pepa and other feminist rappers, I don't mean to suggest that they are entirely exemplary, but that their work merits critical attention for the forms of oppression they do counter. This moment shows that even when racism and sexism are dealt with, there are still other prejudices to be overcome.

Rap's emphasis on lyrics also tailors it to a political agenda, for listening to the words requires thoughtful attention. As Pepa said about other rappers, "You have to listen to their tapes like a hundred times." These particular rap artists are so clear and forthright in their feminist message that you don't have to listen many times to hear them assert their right to control their own bodies.

Because so much of contemporary performance is visual, music videos and long-form music videos such as filmed concerts provide a perfect opportunity for the discussion and analysis of rap. Music videos have also provided the mechanism for rap artists to reach a wide and varied audience. Through shows like *Pump It Up*, hosted by Dee Barnes on Fox Television, *Rap City* on Black Entertainment Television, and *Yo MTV Raps,* rappers have extended their influence and communicated their sense of style, and, in the case of female rappers, their feminist message. While not every female rapper is feminist, and certainly the degree and explicitness of their feminism varies, by virtue of their appearance in a male-dominated and misogynist genre, female rappers militate against sexism and for women.

A 1991 pay-per-view special (cost $19.95) entitled "Sisters in the Name of Rap," which was also released for sale, provides an excellent overview of the contributions of women in rap. This special emphasizes the degree to which a large number of women artists are turning rap to their own ends. Both music videos and pay-per-view customarily bombard the viewer with shots of women used as sexual objects for a male gaze; rap music videos by men feature scantily clad, gyrating female dancers, and the most popular events on pay-per-view are soft porn movies. In this context, then, a two-hour concert by women performers, which might in itself seem unremarkable, creates a radical discontinuity in the televisual text.

"Sisters in the Name of Rap," containing performances by more than twenty-two artists, could really be considered a long-form music video. The concert depicted was clearly played for the cameras and has been edited. It includes a touching tribute to MC Trouble, who was scheduled to perform at this show, but who died suddenly and unexpectedly. A connecting link in the program is the use of two female video jockeys, Dee Barnes (well known for filing a suit against a male rapper who assaulted her), and, backstage, Dutcheez. While this structure is in itself empowering to women because they are in charge of the show, the real connection to feminism lies in the commitment to women that undergirds each performance. Many of the performers echo Nikki Nicole, who announces that she is dedicating her song "to all the black females who came here tonight." Her rap "I Believe in Me" makes the feminist inclinations of the show clear. She espouses female self-affirmation and strength. Attired in a shiny black patent leather coat and backed by a wall of video monitors depicting her visage, Nikki Nicole proclaims, "I will achieve for the fact I believe in me." The visual images reinforce the idea of her self-assurance and autonomy. The backdrop first depicts an immense image of her and then two columns of her image, facing and singing to herself. This refraction is then directed to the audience when the lyrics switch to "just say to yourself

I believe in me." Nikki Nicole's self-assertion is perfectly consonant with the conventions of rap, but, in its switch to promoting the listener, it moves toward the women in the audience to whom she has dedicated the song. In her inclusiveness and attentiveness to women listeners, Nikki Nicole reflects an attitude taken by many female rappers.

Nikki Nicole's self-promotion and confidence is echoed later in the program when Tam Tam proclaims, "There's no limit to the things I can do." Her self-promotion is shored up by the costumes—her musicians and dancers wear T-shirts that proclaim "Tam Tam." In her strong, energetic performance, she persuades the viewers that, as she says "I won't stop until I'm number one." Her ascendancy results in part from the vigorous dance through which she leads her backup dancers. Similarly, Roxanne Shante directs her male dancers through their gyrations and uses Grand Daddy IU, a male rapper, to describe her as "the originator, the first female." She herself declares, "I'm the Queen of Rap and I've mastered it." Yet as she promotes herself, she advises the audience, "Do whatever you do best."

Described as "hip hop's first self-proclaimed feminist activist" (Morgan 1991, 75), Yo-Yo repeats the strong assertions of competency and worth when she declares, "I'm intelligent—I know it," and also insists, "Don't call me baby." Her strong feminist pronouncements are supported by her activism. She founded the Intelligent Black Woman's Coalition, "dedicated to raising self-esteem and dealing with issues like teen pregnancy and drug use among young women. Yo-Yo started the IBWC because she wanted to extend the peer-counseling work she did in her South Central Los Angeles high school to her rap career" (McDonnell, 32–33). Yo-Yo's attire emphasizes that she is a self beyond sexual posturing. While female rappers may wear bustiers and stretch pants and point their posteriors toward the audience, their costumes are characterized by large, loose-fitting jackets that cover up or minimize the exposure of their flesh. Their clothes look comfortable and practical for the strenuous dancing they perform as they rap. Their bodies are not compartmentalized or fetishized as in so many rap videos by male performers (or, for that matter, in other music videos by male and female rock performers). Their dress, then, accentuates both their lyrics and their assertion of a self beyond sexual appeal. Yo-Yo and Nikki Nicole in particular are large women, quite unlike the more customary female rock performers, such as the self-exposing and body-exploiting Madonna.

While these performers downplay their sexuality, Salt 'n Pepa represent another, more specific, manifestation of female strength and energy. Through their lyrics, style and dance, these female rappers emphasize Audre Lorde's "uses of the erotic; the erotic as power" (53). Lorde describes how the erotic can be developed as a strength rather than as a liability for women. If women are in control of their own sexuality and attractiveness, the erotic can be empowering. While all music video performers allude to or use sexuality to promote themselves, Salt 'n Pepa do so explicitly and overtly, but without demeaning themselves or their viewers. They take great relish in depicting female desire for sex through both lyrics and performance. In "Most Men are Tramps," for example, Salt 'n Pepa ask, "Have you ever seen a man who's stupid and rude . . . who thinks he's God's gift to women?" They gesture to the male dancers and demand,

"Don't hand me a line." The rap is highlighted by a group of male dancers wearing trenchcoats. As Salt 'n Pepa repeat "tramp," the dancers flash open their coats to reveal g-strings. Through a clever and playful role reversal, Salt 'n Pepa point to the ways in which male sexuality can be corrupt and unappealing. The male dancers are only exposed for a split second, so they are not trying to exploit the male body, except to make a point. The exposé of male dominance is further emphasized by the band that backs up the group. In a startling contrast to most rap bands, the musicians are all female, and they are attired in jeans and T-shirts. The emphasis is on their musicianship rather than their bodies.

In "Do You Really Want Me?" Salt 'n Pepa press the male characters for an honest answer to that question and, in the process, assert the right of a woman to say no to sex and to her right to control the time and place and circumstances of sexual relations. They advise the audience, "Get to know each other" and then direct the lyrics to themselves: "Be my friend, not just my lover . . . know my mind, not just my body." A male rapper feeds her lines as he pretends to seduce Salt 'n Pepa. He asks if anything is going to happen, and she says, "Nothing." In a segue into "Let's Talk About Sex," they call again for open, honest discussion of sexuality between men and women. They depict the conflict as one between sex and love, and call for a reconciliation between men and women. Pepa asserts her right to talk about sex, even on television, because "everybody has sex." This point in the dialogue prepares the viewer for the words to follow, and the rappers declare that "people who think it's dirty have a choice to change the station." Salt insists that "everybody should be making love." Pepa agrees, but asks, "How many fellows you know make love?" Her intonation and expression make it clear that this is a rhetorical question—that a general failing of men is their attitudes toward sex and women.

The performance directs the viewers' attention toward Salt 'n Pepa's sexual assertiveness. They caress themselves symbolically as male dancers then imitate the motions. As Salt 'n Pepa assert their right to a healthy vibrant sexuality under their own control, Yo-Yo too elicits the image of a woman with desires she considers appropriate. Raising an issue about status that is very much a part of feminist rap, she declares, "You may say I'm not ladylike, but I'm a lady." This reclamation of the term "lady" asserts that women are ladies even if they express sexual desire. Whether one is a "lady" is not to be decided by others but by the woman herself.

The word "lady" appears frequently in feminist rap, but nowhere more effectively than in Queen Latifah's rap, "Ladies First." Queen Latifah uses the plural, ladies, to emphasize female solidarity and sisterhood. In her introduction of Queen Latifah, Dee Barnes identifies "Ladies First" as "the anthem for all the sisters out there." Latifah's version of this song appropriately ends the concert, for it is a song about female solidarity. The music video is discussed extensively in chapter 7, but Queen Latifah's performance deserves special consideration here, for in this film she reformulates her message slightly. The music video that she performed had visuals of historical figures, newsreel footage from South Africa, and a backup chorus of other female rappers. In this performance, however, she directs herself to the audience—in particular, to the women. She calls the women to join her in the refrain. "Sing it with me, girls," she requests, and the camera stresses her relationship with the women in the audience as it zooms in for close-ups of four or five women in the front row, not once, but three times. Like Salt 'n Pepa, Queen Latifah calls for a new type of relationship between men and women. Before her next rap, "Fly Girl," she asks the women in the audience: "How many girls out here have gone into a club or something and passed some guys who said 'Hey baby come here?'" She describes her witty response to situations like that, but then sympathizes briefly with men. She explains that sexist behavior hurts them, too: "I know a lot of guys who are sick of looking bad and getting no place because girls expect them to say stupid nonsense like that." The rap, though, emphasizes women's oppression in dating situations. Responding to a hypothetical pass in a scene she depicts at a club, she raps, "No, my name ain't 'yo' and I ain't got your baby." She goes on, "It's hard to keep a good woman down, so I keep coming." She explains, "But I'm not the type of girl that you think I am; I don't jump into the arms of every man," insisting, "I don't need your money," and demanding, "Treat me like a lady." Echoing Salt 'n Pepa's line, she says, "I want a friend not just a lover." The emphasis on respect and equality appears repeatedly in rap by women. Their demands are clear and unequivocal. Here "Sisters in the Name of Rap" reflects Tricia Rose's description of female rappers' emphasis on heterosexual courtship (1994, 173). The stress on friendship and the emphasis on relationship rather than sex is underscored by Queen Latifah's attire, which, like that of other female rap performers, is modest, especially by the standards of the women who appear with male rappers. She sports a black turban, a large thigh-length beige jacket and black stretch pants. A large woman,

Queen Latifah is elegant and has a commanding presence. She doesn't need to exploit her body to sell her music. Instead, her message itself is sufficient. In a way, "Ladies First" can be considered the message of the show, for the credits roll with this song, and the viewer is treated to brief images of each of the performers.

Queen Latifah, Salt 'n Pepa, Yo-Yo and other female rappers are quite clear about the feminism of their image and rap. As Salt 'n Pepa said in an MTV interview, they "dress the way we want to dress and say what we want to say." Yo-Yo explains in the same MTV rockumentary on rap that "I get to tell the women's side—you know, of how women feel and disagree on some things that males say." Perhaps the most explicit and eloquent of all is Queen Latifah, who, also in the documentary, explains, "Of course, I think we can act as an instrument of change. I think it's important that we do try to change people's concept of how male-female relationships should be." She and the other feminist rappers are doing a superb job of communicating the idea that men and women should interact as equals, that women deserve respect, and that women have a right to sexual desire and gratification.

"Sisters in the Name of Rap," then, provides a nice synecdoche of the feminism expressed in women's rap. There are many different ways of expressing feminism, but while the emphases may vary, the central concerns of female autonomy and respect for women do not change. This brief survey of female rappers, I hope, begins to suggest that popular culture, even an overtly misogynist genre like rap, can provide a place for feminist sentiments to flourish. Female rappers can be seen as yet another triumph for African-American women, who, in popular music as well as in the written word, express unparalleled creativity. This concert video also suggests the ways in which dress and style can be used to augment and underscore a message delivered in words. Most important, the presence of dozens of women rappers together in concert is a testament to African-American women's strength and power.

Cornel West argues, "Black musical practices—packaged via radio or video, records or live performance—are oppositional in the weak sense that they keep alive some sense of the agency and creativity of oppressed peoples" (96). Feminist rappers are oppositional in more than this sense; they specifically draw our attention to sexism and racism and present a model for their viewers of ways to act.

So much of what has been written about rap has proclaimed the genre's misogyny that no one who has only heard of artists like Public Enemy or 2 Live Crew or N. W. A. would expect rap to contain as well feminist performers like M. C. Lyte, Queen Latifah or Salt 'n Pepa. Yet while Michelle Wallace can write that "[l]ike many black feminists I look on sexism in rap as a necessary evil," she can also acknowledge that the answer to "the tensions between the sexes in the black community . . . may lie with women" rappers. She says that "feminist criticism, like many other forms of social analysis, is widely considered part of hostile white culture" (1990b, C11). Rap music, like all other forms of popular music, is innately neither feminist nor political; nevertheless, female performers have excelled in using rap's specific generic qualities to promote feminist messages of self-assertion for women, the necessity of a strong identity for women, the legitimacy of women's sexual desires, and explicit criticism of sexism. Feminist rap should be considered and evaluated as practical feminist criticism.

This is the appropriate preface for a close textual and visual analysis of one feminist music video, Queen Latifah's "Ladies First." This chapter and the next demonstrate that feminist rap music videos are a rich, resistant genre emerging from contemporary music. Examining both feminist rappers as a group and one stellar example of a feminist music video reveals the feminist community that is a powerful part of popular culture.

Chapter Seven

"Ladies First": Queen Latifah's Afrocentric Video

We have to learn to fight racism, sexism, and homophobia. You gotta fight all three at the same time.　　　　　—Queen Latifah

By examining "Ladies First" closely, this chapter explores in detail the issues raised by feminist rap, which is rap that focuses on promoting women's importance, that demands equal treatment for women, and that demonstrates the need for women to support each other. While the politics of entertainment are often troubling and ambivalent, there are feminist entertainments, like "Ladies First," that present the viewer with moments of resistance to dominant exploitative images of women. In its serious exploration and glorification of African-American women's history, "Ladies First" seizes a televisual moment and breaks the continuity of sexism and racism that dominates the music video flow. While "Ladies First" is not completely and unambiguously feminist, there is a coherence to the images and lyrics that contrasts strikingly not only with music videos by male performers but also even with music videos like "Sisters Are Doin' It For Themselves," performed by Aretha Franklin and Annie Lennox. In Franklin and Lennox's video, for example, arbitrary, unconnected and traditional portraits of women undercut rather than strengthen the overtly feminist message of the lyrics.

By contrast, the complexity of the lyrics and images of "Ladies First" refutes the notion that popular culture texts will inevitably and exclusively exploit gender and Afrocentricity (if these concepts even appear at all).

Significantly, "Ladies First" draws upon postmodernism to accentuate its Afrocentric bent. This music video, like other feminist videos, uses the postmodern aspects of the form—fragmentation, pastiche, self-reflexivity and a breakdown between genres—to make explicit political statements about race and gender. As we have seen, rap itself is postmodern, and thus well suited to take advantage of television's postmodern form, the music video.

Queen Latifah's feminism draws on the patterns of rap discussed in the previous chapter to assert the importance of women promoting themselves and other women. She is able to use the form without being accused of being self-centered or narcissistic.[1] In "Ladies First," Queen Latifah touts herself as a "perfect specimen," and Monie Love (aka Simone Johnson) spells out her professional name, which suggests the paradox of the conjunction of love and money in a capitalist society. Love's name draws attention to the nature of the music business, which so frequently uses the notion of love to make money. These feminist rappers' names make their wry understanding of capitalism clear and should allay any doubts about their awareness of the complexities and ambiguities of their position. Queen Latifah's CD, *All Hail the Queen*, "reached number 6 on the R&B charts and sold over a million copies" (Gaar 422).

Through her name and what she emphasizes, Queen Latifah draws upon a tradition of African music and culture to make her criticism of sexism and racism. She was born Dana Owens in East Orange, New Jersey. The name Latifah, which means "delicate and sensitive" in Arabic, was conferred upon her by a friend, and suggests the Afrocentric nature of her performances. (She added "Queen" herself when she became a professional rapper.) Angela Davis explains that "according to African tradition, one's name is supposed to capture the essence of one's being" (Davis 100). Because of this tradition, Dick Hebdige asserts, names have particular power in Afrocentric music: "Naming can be in and of itself an act of invocation, conferring power and grace upon the namer: the names can carry power in themselves. The titles bestowed on Haile Selassie in a Rastafarian chant or reggae toast or on James Brown or Aretha Franklin in a soul toast or MC rap testify to this power . . . the namer pays tribute in the 'name check' to the community from which (s)he has sprung and without which (s)he would be unable to survive" (8). Similarly, Queen Latifah promotes herself as a rapper, a toast to herself that is part of the rap tradition.[2]

Queen Latifah's Afrocentricity occurs in the music as well as in her use of names and images. The rhythms of rap are those of Africa. As Hebdige describes it, there is a substantial difference between European music and African music: "African, Afro-American and Caribbean music is based on quite different principles from the European classical tradition . . . Rhythm and percussion play a much more central role. In the end there is a link in these non-European musics with public life, with speech, with textures and grains of the living human voice" (12). Drawing on African and African-American traditions of music as resistance,[3] Queen Latifah transforms these qualities into rap to criticize racism. Like many male rappers, Latifah subscribes to the belief that black North Americans must look to Africa in order to create their identities and culture, saying, "To me Afrocentricity is a way of living. . . . It's about being into yourself and into your people and being proud of your origins." She attributes her interest and knowledge to her "very cultured family" who were "very aware" of African culture (Dafoe D8). (Her mother is a high school history teacher.) Through her use of beat and language, she promotes women and attacks apartheid.

Significantly, she does so by using the very forms that are used (by many male rappers) to denigrate women, thus reclaiming it for women. At the same time, by using rap and Afrocentricity, she asserts the centrality of women to an Afrocentric outlook. Being feminist does not mean abandoning her African heritage; instead, it becomes an additional source of strength and power. Her attire in particular reveals the way in which an African-based clothing style can assert an eroticism that resists the nakedness and exposure of Western styles for women (such as the dresses and high heels worn by Tina Turner).

Queen Latifah's Afrocentricity operates both culturally and politically. Her regality, her name, and her self-promotion associate her with a tradition of African royalty. Through her attire, she draws attention to styles and colors that are associated with Africa. Her military dress and the colors that she wears (red, black and green) suggest the African National Congress. Scenes in the video depict armed struggle in South Africa, emphasizing that, in her case, style is used to underscore a political message. In the video, Queen Latifah's Afrocentricity is also apparent in her neonationalistic positioning of herself as a leader of African-American men and women rappers. Queen Latifah appropriates rap, politicizes it, and uses it to promote herself and other African-American women.

Latifah's use of Afrocentricity makes her work part of a debate about postmodernism and its relation to African-American culture. African-American culture is a part of the creation of postmodernism, just as modernism involved an appropriation of forms such as jazz and sculpture from African-American culture.

By employing the strategies of postmodernism inherent in the music video form, Queen Latifah forces viewers to question the assumption that complexity and linguistic play only exist in high art produced by white men. Her video exemplifies Houston Baker's description of rap as "the form of audition in our present era that utterly refuses to sing anthems of, say, white male hegemony" (1990a, 182). By using Afrocentric images and style in a postmodern art form, "Ladies First" requires its viewers to accept the overlap between two apparently distinct cultural phenomena. While Afrocentricity looks to Africa as a source of unity and historical continuity, postmodernism emphasizes fragmentation and contradiction. In "Ladies First," however, the two are linked together in the service of Queen Latifah's trenchant critique of racism and sexism. Although Afrocentrism and postmodernism are implicated in sexism, her text implies, both can be redeemed if used carefully. Through the video images and words of her rap, Queen Latifah creates a unified, but far from seamless, sense of the intersection of the perspectives of Afrocentrism, postmodernism, and feminism. Examining her music video in detail allows us to see magnified the relationships between South Africa and the United States, between performance and resistance, and between history and contemporary politics.

As the previous chapter demonstrates, feminist rap videos point to the ways in which systems of oppression are interdependent. They do so by drawing on the possibilities of the music video form, which allows one message to be communicated through the lyrics while another, complementary, message can be carried through images. While performers like (The Real) Roxanne, Salt 'n Pepa, and M. C. Lyte have made explicitly feminist music videos, these videos do not draw specifically on Afrocentricity or the feminist solidarity that Queen Latifah uses (see Keyes; Roberts 1991, 141–52). More important, these videos are not as explicitly political and do not challenge the structure of commercial music. The feminist message of "Ladies First" is particularly powerful in the context of the other videos that air on MTV and BET. This feminist video stands out in marked contrast to the sexist videos that frame it; its message, which might seem moderate in other contexts, is here a compelling challenge to the dominant patriarchal social order. Queen Latifah's music video is notable among other feminist videos, including feminist rap videos, because of her use of women's history and women's biography, two traditional feminist strategies.

Queen Latifah's success, however, is framed by the limitations that she accepts—her music video, like almost all music videos, accepts the premises of compulsory heterosexuality. Despite her public statement against homophobia, this particular music video remains well inside the frame of compulsory heterosexuality. While she examines sexism and racism, she does not question the code of heterosexual relationships that underlies

most of the products advertised on MTV and BET. Since
I know of only one music video that does ("I Kissed a
Girl" discussed in chapter 2), it may be that this limita-
tion is embedded in the commercial music video form.
Perhaps even radical commercials remain constrained by
the advertising need that generated the form.

Although popular culture limits the possibility of radicalism in music videos, however, this form provides a
unique opportunity for an Afrocentric feminist rapper.
For example, it was Latifah's demo video, "Princess of the
Posse," shown on MTV, which led to her contract with
Tommy Boy Records (Kennedy). This history reverses
the old pattern in which a performer got a contract
and then produced a music video. Rap music videos can
be seen daily on a special MTV program, *Yo MTV Raps*
(which, according to Jon Pareles, "consistently draws
the cable channel's largest audiences, proving that rap
appeals to fans a long way from its early strongholds
in black urban neighborhoods" [28]), and on *Rap City*,
an hour-long show on BET. Both shows frequently air
music videos by female performers, and Queen Latifah,
Sweet Tee, and Antoinette have been guests on *Rap City*.
As Antoinette points out about music videos, "That's
how you get into the groove of it and also it helps the
song because when a person sees your video they get a
picture of what's going on, so a video definitely helps."
A music video "helps" rap artists in particular, because
many radio stations refuse to play rap songs. Music videos
have enabled dozens of women rap artists to get attention and promote their records. More important for
feminist rappers, music videos provide the opportunity
to underscore their feminist message by offering alternative, positive images of women that contradict the

stereotypical images of African-American women such as those identified by the Combahee River Collective in "A Black Feminist Statement": "mammy, matriarch, Saphire, whore, bulldagger" (13–14).

Furthermore, rap is uniquely accessible to feminist appropriation. Because rap is still a relatively undercapitalized venture, rap artists have far more control over their videos—their product—than new artists starting out with major record labels. For example, Antoinette's video "Shake, Rattle and Roll" was filmed in fourteen hours; Queen Latifah's was finished in twenty-two hours. While "Ladies First" is polished and professional, it was devised by Queen Latifah, Monie Love and Shakim, Queen Latifah's manager, in a London hotel room. In Queen Latifah's words, there "we sat, revised and rewrote the whole thing." In a music video, a feminist rapper can extend and solidify the message of the lyrics. Latifah explains that "Ladies First" was written to "lift females up." She continues, "[W]e wrote the concept for the video and I wanted female rappers in to show a unified thing" ("Much Music"). The "unified thing"—a group of female rappers singing "ladies first" in unison—is more compelling on the video, where the viewer can actually identify the various artists who are working with Latifah, than on the track, when their personalities are indistinct. This is an example of how a music video can augment and intensify a feminist message and its importance for African-American women. Here too Latifah shares with other African-American women writers what Michael Awkward has described as "the figure of a common (female) tongue, of a shared Afro-American woman's authorial voice" (13). While Queen Latifah's vision is not the only possible Afrocentric feminist agenda, her music video is part of a continuum of Afrocentric feminism promulgated by Alice Walker, Zora Neale Hurston and other African-American women artists.

The range of African and African-American feminism is stressed by the first frames of the music video. "Ladies First" opens with slides of four women: three African-American political activists—Madam C. J. Walker, Sojourner Truth, and Angela Davis—and an African political activist, the young Winnie Mandela. To emphasize Queen Latifah's connection to these women, the pictures are repeated later in the video, with Latifah proudly singing in front of them. (Later images include Harriet Tubman and a still of Cicely Tyson playing Tubman in the film *A Woman Called Moses*.) Queen Latifah and Monie Love begin singing "Ladies First" with the backdrop of a bombed-out housing project and the river looming in the background. Their singing is accompanied by the frenetic dancing of the Safari Sisters, attired in bright yellow-and-black jackets and wearing black boots. Interspersed with these frames is news footage from South Africa depicting the armed struggle against apartheid. In counterpoint, Queen Latifah appears as a military strategist using a pointer to remove giant white chess pieces and replacing them with black power fists. Twice as the chorus "ladies first" is sung, we see a line of prominent feminist rappers in close-up. The video ends with a darkened skyline and Queen Latifah proclaiming "ladies first."

"Ladies First" exemplifies the possibilities of the music video form for feminist artists and the sophistication of Queen Latifah's work. The play on the chivalric phrase "ladies first" is clever, sophisticated and multilayered. Until the twentieth century, the phrase would not, of course, have been used to refer to African-American women. Its reclamation here positions Latifah as a lady, a rank underscored by her assumption of the title "queen," with which she links herself to a heritage of African queens. The irony of the phrase is that while "ladies" were supposed to be "first," their status was completely titular; they had no legal rights or powers.

The words can also be interpreted literally. Latifah, Monie Love and the other female rappers are putting themselves first and promoting themselves as performers. Here they draw on rap's focus on self-promotion to make a feminist statement. Furthermore, they are doing so collaboratively. The conjunction with the scenes of South Africa, including scenes of women fighting and of Latifah knocking figures off the war map and replacing them with the clenched fist that symbolizes the struggle against racism, suggests yet another reading of the words "ladies first." Here the lyric implies that women can and should be first in revolution, a claim underscored by the slides of notable African-American freedom fighters like Harriet Tubman and Angela Davis.

Most compellingly, the juxtaposition of the phrase "ladies first" with the scenes from South Africa points up the hypocrisy of arguments for separate spheres for men and women or whites and blacks, showing how the same rationales are used to justify the oppression of blacks and of women, and identifying the similarity between sexism and racism and the importance of resisting both. Through the parallel structure of lyrics/images, which is unique to music videos, Latifah can draw on her dual heritage of Afrocentricity and African-American feminism to depict sexism and racism as related. As she does her interest in Afrocentricity, Latifah attributes her interest in feminism to her parents. Through her music she hopes to "lift females up," explaining that "I got that message from my parents" ("Much Music"). Her heritage extends beyond her biological family, however, as we see from the series of slides that begins the video.

The photographs and pictures provide a history of Latifah's African-American lineage. Through the images of African-American women who fought for freedom for women and blacks, she suggests that, in a number of different ways, women have been and should be in the forefront of struggles against both forms of oppression.[4] The sequence also points up how this aspect of history is unappreciated and omitted from curriculums. When I first saw the video, I was able to recognize only Truth, Davis and Tubman, and, significantly, Rose does not mention Walker in her discussion of the video either. Staring at the pictures over and over again, I realized how ignorant I am of African-American women's history. By beginning with these unidentified slides, Latifah makes each viewer aware of her knowledge or lack of knowledge about African-American "ladies." As Latifah herself says, "I wanted to show the strength of black women in history—strong black women. Those were good examples. I wanted to show what we've done. We've done a lot, it's just that people don't know it. Sisters have been in the midst of these things for a long time, but we just don't get to see it that much" (Rose 1990, 19). The opening works as a hook, to pull the viewer into the video, and it also makes the viewer think about what each woman stands for and how Latifah herself fits into this lineage.

The video opens with a slide of Madam C. J. Walker, a millionaire cosmetics manufacturer. Although she might seem like an unusual choice for the first image in a feminist music video, Walker nicely encapsulates Latifah's dual message about art and rebellion. With a formula that she created, Walker built an empire based on cosmetic products for black women. She used her wealth to endow a school for girls in West Africa, and she donated large sums of money to African-American institutions and charities (Robinson 138). As Paula Giddings writes, Walker's "will stipulated that two thirds of her fortune go to various charities, and that her company always be controlled by a woman" (Giddings 188). Giddings praises Walker for employing thousands of black women and for improving their lives. By putting "ladies first," Walker made a fortune, lived lavishly and was widely admired for her success and flamboyant social life. She can thus be viewed as an early African-American celebrity. The appellation "Madam" suggests the esteem in which she was held; being herself a queen of sorts, she was a precursor for Queen Latifah. Like Latifah, Walker was adept at self-promotion, and her marketing of her own image qualifies her as a performer in popular culture. In a striking action that recalls Sojourner Truth, Walker, after being denied a place on the program of the 1912 National Negro Business League Convention, stood up and addressed the audience. She so impressed them that she was invited to be the keynote speaker the following year (Hine 1211).

The second slide shows Sojourner Truth, a former slave and an eloquent and famous speaker. Given the name Isabella, Truth renamed herself in the African tradition of naming identified by Davis. Truth's name does reflect the essence of her inner being, as does Latifah's over a century later. Truth attended the Second National Women's Suffrage Convention and riveted those in attendance when she alone challenged the male ministers who were praising the male intellect and dominating the conference. She met with Lincoln and is perhaps best known for her speech "Ain't I a Woman," which links racism and sexism and depicts this double oppression faced by black women (Bennett and Bogin). Truth is important to many contemporary African-American feminists like bell hooks, whose first book on feminism is entitled *Ain't I a Woman*. Truth's verbal capabilities make her another precursor for a feminist rapper like Latifah, for Truth proved through her speech that words do have the power to challenge sexism and racism and to alter people's visions of reality. Like Truth, Latifah challenges male authority; through this association, Latifah emphasizes her own Afrocentric feminist position.

With the third slide, Angela Davis, Latifah raises a number of issues, including that of class. The move from a millionaire capitalist to a former slave to a woman who writes about gender, race and class reminds the viewers of the importance of class and of rap's positioning in capitalism. Angela Davis is easily the most radical of the references, because she is a card-carrying Communist Party militant.

Like Madam Walker's cosmetics, rap has created and supported a number of African-American record companies and made fortunes for some of its practitioners. Like Walker herself, Latifah has the prospect of making a great deal of money from her work. By showing Davis in this series, Latifah seems to be both endorsing entrepreneurship and also warning about how class divides and oppresses. The inclusion of Davis, a critic of capitalism, a writer and an agitator for civil rights and women's rights, allows Latifah to point to the interdependence of different kinds of oppression and the necessity of fighting on all fronts. Like Truth, Davis writes about herself—her autobiography is a powerful exposé of racism and sexism in the United States. Connecting herself with Davis indicates Latifah's desire to be associated with radicalism and also emphasizes that Latifah is a writer; rap is, after all, a writerly text. Davis is also a professor, so Latifah makes explicit the didactic function of her art by including this picture of Davis in the opening of the video.[5] Moving from an image of a woman in the nineteenth-century to one of Davis in the twentieth emphasizes that there are still battles to be waged against racism and sexism. The trajectory is optimistic, because the sequence of Walker to Truth and then Davis indicates that African-American women are attacking oppression in increasingly powerful and direct ways. While Davis was acquitted of murder, kidnapping and conspiracy charges after her gun was used to kill a judge, her image evokes the notion of violence used in self-defense, an issue directly raised in South Africa, where the African National Congress is pledged to use whatever means necessary to end apartheid. Violence is present in the video, too, in the compelling image of a woman lying dead after a demonstration in South Africa. The cost of fighting for freedom is high, as Winnie Mandela, who appears in the fourth slide, well knows.

Following Davis with Mandela indicates a contemporary connection as African and African-American women struggle against sexism and racism. Both Davis and Mandela have written autobiographies that reveal the systems of oppression in their countries, and Davis has a chapter on Mandela in her book of critical essays, *Women, Culture and Politics*. The picture of a young Winnie Mandela reminds us of the long history of struggle against apartheid and of how she managed to keep the African

National Congress alive and visible despite her husband's lengthy imprisonment and her own banning and house arrest. The portrait of a jeweled and elegant Mandela reinforces descriptions of her as "a woman of regal presence" (Lelyvald 211) and as possessing "spiritual beauty and political eloquence" (Davis 98). The juxtaposition of Davis and Mandela suggests that struggles against racism and sexism are international and reminds us of America's involvement in South Africa and our responsibility to resist racism throughout the world.

It remains for Latifah to take the combination of art and politics to the next logical step. In doing so, she realizes Angela Davis's description of music's radical potential: "Black people were able to create with their music an aesthetic community of resistance, which in turn encouraged and nurtured a political community of active struggle for freedom" (201). Latifah draws on a heritage of African-American womanhood, positioning herself and her music video as logical successors in the tradition of struggle against racism and sexism. Art and politics are paired again in the video when Latifah stands proudly in front of a slide of Harriet Tubman, a legendary escaped slave who helped hundreds of other slaves get to freedom. Moments later, the slide changes to a depiction of Cicely Tyson playing Tubman in A Woman Called Moses. In this series, Latifah asserts the centrality, power and responsibility of art to refresh our memories about African-American women's history and the need to continue the struggle—especially, according to this video, against apartheid in South Africa. The slides of African-American women explicate the South African footage without a word about South Africa or apartheid being used in the rap lyrics.

The use of historical photographs and news footage from South Africa enhances Latifah's message. In these scenes, one of two glimpses of men in the video, women fight alongside men. Through these images, which range from black-and white-pictures to color film, she points to the length of the struggle against racism, providing encouragement with the allusions to successful women leaders like Harriet Tubman. The grim newsreels reveal how much there is yet to combat. The video makes the movement from life to art and back again, connecting history (the slides of African-American women) to the events of the more recent newsreels (armed struggle in South Africa) to the symbolic enactment of resistance to art itself, the rap music video. Through her actions and her attire, Latifah clearly identifies herself as a participant in the struggle. Sporting a sash with African National Congress colors, Latifah destroys figures on the board map of South Africa and leads a group of men to clench their fists and vow to continue the struggle. This moment shows that men and women must work together to fight apartheid.

The message of cooperation is strengthened by the way in which the video is shot to emphasize the lyrics. The images of women singing in chorus vividly convey the idea of cooperation, in contrast to rap's traditional emphasis on the individual competing with and denigrating other rappers. Throughout the music video, Latifah and Monie Love engage in conversation. Like another feminist rap group, Salt 'n Pepa, Latifah and Monie rap in dialogue. In this regard they differ from many male rappers, who engage the mike solitarily. Monie and Latifah ask each other before one of them takes over the mike. For example, Monie asks Queen, "Hey yo let me take it from here,

Queen," as the camera pans from her face to Latifah's face and back again. She concludes by saying, "Let me take a position, ladies first, yes?" Her feminine ending reflects women's conversational patterns: women use more tag questions than men, according to Robin Lakoff. She is answered by Latifah's resounding "Yes," and then Latifah continues the rap. They exchange again when Monie asks permission to take the mike—"My sister, can I get some?"—and Latifah responds, "Yeah, Monie Love, grab the mike and get dumb." Their cooperation and artistic collaboration are apparent as the camera moves from one to the other throughout the video and emphasized when they stand right next to each other, faces in profile, chins atilt, with Latifah's hand on Monie's shoulder.

Latifah also resists the traditional subordination of background singers and dancers in her use of the autonomous Safari Sisters, the dancers in the video. Such performers are frequently women, and they are customarily depicted in music videos as sex objects. The Safari Sisters, on the other hand, have their own identity; they choose their own outfits, which are vivid and engaging but not revealing—jackets, shorts and boots and design their own dances. Through their coordinated gyrations, they underscore the message of sisterhood. They appear to dance primarily with each other. As Latifah said on *Rap City*, "They do their own thing." Their stage names, 007 and 99, accentuate the play with militarism that characterizes Latifah's stance. By referring to films (James Bond) and to television (*Get Smart*), they call to mind both mediums and playfully appropriate the signifiers from white men for their struggles. At the end of the video, they clasp their hands to make an arch for Latifah. In this concluding gesture, they visually support her call: "ladies first." Further, the inclusion of a number of other female rappers in the music video stresses sisterhood. As a group including Antoinette, Ms. Melodie, Ice Cream Tee, and Shelly Thunder sings the chorus, the camera slowly pans their faces. Smiling and laughing they present a visual representation of the words they sing: "ladies first." This scene in particular undercuts rap's competitive nature, in which rappers are obliged to be combative about other rappers. As Tricia Rose explains, "Her decision to collaborate on her debut album is as surprising as it is ambitious; it suggests that being a solo rap artist does mean isolating yourself from your peers" (1991, 16)— especially your female peers. Latifah specifically refutes masculine rap's heightened sense of individualism, both by including other female rappers and by using pictures of women like Tubman and Davis. Latifah knows that women have to work together, and her images and lyrics stress this message. It is in her use of the chorus of female rappers and in her dialogue with Monie Love that Queen Latifah's feminism—her commitment to improve the position of women and to work with other women— is most obvious. While "Ladies First" does criticize male sexism, it also celebrates African-American women as heterosexuals. In this regard, Queen Latifah's music video fails to present an alternative to compulsory hetero- sexuality and neglects another obvious interpretation of "ladies first."

The words of the song are quite explicitly feminist. Latifah and Monie stress women's power as mothers and as artists. Women are "stepping, rhyming, cutting" and "not forgetting we're the ones who give birth." "Like mother, like daughter," Monie states, stressing lineage and the strength of the mother-daughter tie. "I'm the daughter of a sister who is the mother of a brother," she explains, reeling out her connections in familial, matrilineal terms. She calls for "respect due to the mother who's the root of it," a framing expounded upon by Latifah, who concludes the video with a rap about "queens of civilization," an Afrocentric claiming of her heritage and an expansion of the idea of mothering to include cultures. With this phrase, she reminds her viewers of the pivotal role Africa has played in the development of human civilization. Women's strength also enhances their artistry. Latifah proclaims that "the ladies will kick at a rhyme that is wicked," and Monie praises "all the beats and rhymes my sisters have applied." Latifah depicts her work as "laying down track after track waiting for the climax / When I get there that's when I attacks." This spirited phrasing reminds us of her military attire and position against sexism and racism. The CD alone might make it seem as though the lines refer only to music, but with the augmentation of images the "attack" becomes multilayered. Latifah stresses her own power when she attributes to herself the qualities not only of a lady and a queen but also of a goddess: "I'm divine and my mind expands throughout the universe." While to those unfamiliar with rap, this statement might sound grandiose, in the context of rap, in which self-aggrandizement is expected, it is a modest claim and one that promotes other women at the same time. She declares herself representative of womanhood and shares her power and screen time with other women, who are a part of her universe. She connects her feminist power to the pleasure of the audience. "Grab the mike look at the crowd and see smiles because they see a woman standing on her own two." Or as Monie puts it: "Believe me when

I say being a woman is great / All the fellows out there agree with me." Like her the viewer can be "merrily, merrily . . . overjoyed / Pleased with all the beats and rhymes my sisters have applied."

Their job involves promoting an Afrocentric image of strong womanhood. They assert feminine strength and power. "A woman can bear you, break you, take you," Latifah warns. She and Monie take upon themselves the responsibility of explicating gender relations for their listeners. "So listen very carefully as I break it down for you," Love insists. "Believe me when I say being a woman's great." Monie's positivism is counterpointed by Latifah's bluntness: "Who said the ladies couldn't make it must be blind / If you don't believe well here listen to my rhyme." They speak together, disparaging sexists, demanding that "stereotypes they got to go." Their rhymes are accentuated by their attire, which suggests power through the military and regal appurtenances: Monie in black, wearing a beret and boots, Latifah dressed like a general. In one scene, she wears a white jacket with military fringe. An extreme close-up shows her prominent turban, which connects her to Africa and also to the historical African-American women in the slides that open the video. Latifah's and Monie's powerful screen presence persuasively underscores the rap's message. As the video concludes, viewers are told, "You get the drift, it's ladies first."

This dramatic and powerful rendering of an African-American feminist message through a rap music video shows that even so unpropitious a setting as music videos or rap can be turned to feminist ends. Through her unique combining of an Afrocentric image, music and feminism, Latifah emphasizes the importance of women in African-American culture and in liberation movements,

such as the one taking place in South Africa. By stressing
the strengths of women as mothers and as artists, Latifah
connects the two as mutually empowering. Through her
rap dialogue with Monie Love and the use of a backup
chorus of female rappers, Latifah produces a new interpretation of the expression "ladies first."

Since a music video is brief, Latifah can only hint at
the significance of the African-American women she dis-
plays as forerunners. What would she have her viewers
do? That remains unclear, and even the connection between South Africa and Afrocentricity leaves racism here
in America unconnected to apartheid in South Africa.
Nevertheless, "Ladies First" is still worth studying (and
teaching) because it raises (without resolving) issues of
gender and race, and because it refutes the prevailing
notions of certain popular culture forms as inherently
misogynist and racist.

Like Julie Brown, Queen Latifah has expanded her
career, going on from recording into television, films
and entrepreneurship. One of the stars of a new situation comedy, "Living Single," a huge hit on the Fox
network, Queen Latifah promotes her message of sisterhood in a comedy about the relationship of four
young women living together in New York. While no
explicit mention is made of Queen Latifah's rap career,
the bedroom on her set is decorated with posters from
her CDs, and she "plays a character not that different
from herself" (Meisler 29). Despite the demanding pace
of acting in a television series, Queen Latifah has produced a third CD on Motown Records. Its first single
and video, "U. N. I. T. Y. (Who You Calling a Bitch)"
continues the Afrocentric feminism of "Ladies First." In
"U. N. I. T. Y." Queen Latifah attacks those rappers who

denigrate women, disses sexual harassment and domestic violence, and calls for unity among African-American
men and women. This CD has already gone platinum, and
the track was featured in an episode of "Living Single"
in which the women confronted a man who called them
"bitches."

This extended close analysis of "Ladies First" reveals
that music videos are worthy of feminist attention. While
"Ladies First" would, by any criteria, be an extraordinary
text, there are many other feminist music videos that
merit critical attention. This chapter will, I hope, be read
as an example of the kind of readings that can and should
be done with other music videos. Feminist music videos
explore the issues that are of central importance to feminists: gender and performance, race and gender, postmodernism and feminism, humor and feminism, sexuality
and feminism. Feminist music videos can be used in the
classroom as a tool for educating students about feminist
theories; they can be used to introduce feminism to
friends and neighbors. As a tremendously popular genre,
music videos provide a means of sending feminist ideas to
millions. The success of feminist performers in creating
careers for themselves *and* promulgating feminist ideas
should be an example for all feminists.

Notes

Introduction

1. U 68 was purchased by a cable merchandising company, which replaced music videos with merchandise hawked in stereo sound. Although U 68 no longer exists, its influence continued in MTV's *One Hundred and Twenty Minutes*, *Buzz Clips*, and other shows that highlighted videos by little-known artists and in the greater flexibility in the MTV playlist.

Chapter 1

1. E. Ann Kaplan, pioneering critic of music videos and the author of the first book on MTV (*Rocking Around the Clock: Music Television, Postmodernism and Consumer Culture*), stresses the difficulty of obtaining information about music videos from the channel. Her videography includes the names of only a few directors. As she points out, there is not yet a reference guide for music videos.

Chapter 2

1. See, for example, Aimee Mann's portrayal of a woman finding her own voice in "Voices Carry."

2. A Valley Girl is identified by her use of distinctive slang and her narcissism and materialism. The name comes from the San Fernando Valley, an upper-class part of Southern California.

3. Feminist revisions of fairy tales have a long history; see Jack Zipes, *Don't Bet on the Prince: Contemporary Feminist Fairy Tales in North America and England* for both primary and secondary material.

Chapter 3

1. For example, a study published by the Annenberg School of Communications at the University of Pennsylvania in 1986 claims that sex is more graphic in music videos than on prime time television, and criticizes music videos for a distinctly adolescent slant toward sexuality and for depicting women as sex objects. Similarly, in *The Village Voice*, Barry Walters criticizes the depiction of women, saying that "women on MTV are there to certify the product . . . clips feature carefully cast female fans. . . . It's the good old missionary position being promoted" (40). In a story entitled "Sex as a Weapon" in *Spin*, a rock and roll magazine, Tama Janowitz writes, "Video made them video stars. It made most of them female. Sex is their calling card, but will it also be their downfall?" (54). In a syndicated column, Sue Rusche cites the American Academy of Pediatrics warning about sexually explicit rock music and advises parents to "regulate child's music video viewing" (2C). Music videos are singled out as magnifying the objectionable sexual messages in rock music.

2. At the outset, though, even a champion of music videos must acknowledge that the videos rarely depict anything but heterosexuality. Madonna's notorious "Justify My Love" is a rare mainstream exception.

3. Before I started watching and studying music videos, I sided with Dworkin and MacKinnon, but now I see that there are possibilities for resistance in depictions of sexuality.

4. Andrew Goodwin cites the sales of the music video as being between 400,000 and 500,000 (39). See his discussion of "Justify My Love" (101).

Chapter 5

1. Susan Holly argues that "many find the music comforting compared with the anger and frustration of rap" (33).

Her analysis is echoed by performer Wendy Waldman, who says, "There's no way I'm gonna sing 'wake up wearing nothing but a smile.' Women, unless you're in punk music or rap or some very extreme form of pop music, aren't gonna sing that stuff" (Kingsbury 1992c, 28–29). This attitude toward rap is buttressed by the rarity of African-American country performers and the absence of any acknowledgment of race in song lyrics. Bufwack and Oermann list only a couple of African-American female country music acts (407). Rogers cites only one song with any reference to racial minorities (187–88).

2. See, for example, Melton A. McLaurin's description of country music as a southern art form (16).

3. Holly cites sales figures, the number of record labels in Nashville, the number of radio stations and listeners, and the number two preference for country music in the nation's top one hundred markets.

4. See Rogers (11). Of the top country songs from 1965 to 1980, 73 percent were about love.

5. Examples include "Men," the Forester Sisters; "Company Time," Linda Davis; "He's a Good Ole Boy," Chely Wright; "Blame it On Your Heart," Patty Loveless; "Don't Tell Me What To Do," Pam Tillis; "Passionate Kisses," Mary-Chapin Carpenter; "Janie's Gone Fishin'," Kim Hill; "Walking Away a Winner," Kathy Mattea; "My Night to Howl," Lorrie Morgan; "Silver Thread and Golden Needles," Tammy Wynette, Loretta Lynn, Dolly Parton; "What I Like About You," Trisha Yearwood; "Now I Know," Lari White; "Break Those Chains," Deborah Allen; "Tears Dry," Victora Shaw; and many others.

6. Fenster describes country music videos as eschewing the postmodern qualities of other music videos (114–15).

Chapter 6

1. Their active politics was shown by Queen Latifah with "an announcement geared toward a youth audience in

support of abortion rights—though due to its controversial nature, the PSA was ultimately rejected by MTV and was screened on a few cable networks" (Gaar 441). Salt 'n Pepa have made public service announcements about AIDS and discuss sex and rape in their music videos.

2. Other rap songs express a homophobic attitude. Another glaring example is Tone Loc's "Funky Coal Medina." I certainly agree with bell hooks when she argues that black communities are not more homophobic than other communities, and that, indeed, white communities that refuse to even name homosexuality are more insidious. However, hooks does admit that the black community is perhaps more vocal about expressing homophobic sentiments, and this vocality appears, logically enough, in some rap videos (120–26). This attitude should be compared to Queen Latifah's view: "We, as Black people, are so divided already that we can't afford to annihilate any particular group of ourselves. We have to learn to fight racism, sexism, and homophobia. You gotta fight all three at the same time" (Chambers and Morgan, 118).

Chapter 7

1. A particularly vivid example of this phenomenon is cited by David Toop: "The competitive spirit still flares among b boys (though seemingly less among the b girls). For Bobby Robinson the contradiction is clear: 'Damn it, every group I meet is number one!'" (19).

2. Rap's connection to Afrocentricity is underscored by one of its early major figures, Afrika Bambaata, who, like Queen Latifah, renamed himself, choosing the name of a nineteenth-century Zulu chief.

3. Angela Davis describes music's resistance: "Of all the art forms associated with Afro-American culture, music has played the greatest catalytic role in awakening social consciousness in the community. During the era of slavery,

Black people were victims of a conscious strategy of cultural genocide, which proscribed the practice of virtually all African customs with the exception of music" (200–201).

4. In her sense of African-American women's history, Latifah repeats and reinforces the writings of Angela Davis, bell hooks, and the Combahee River Collective, which writes, "Contemporary Black feminism is the outgrowth of generations of personal sacrifice, militancy, and work by our mothers and sisters."

5. Davis stresses the political dimension of art in *Women, Culture, and Politics*: "Art can function as a sensitizer and catalyst, propelling people toward involvement in organized movements seeking to effect radical social change" (200). While she does mention rap briefly, she does not mention feminist rappers and in an earlier essay speaks disparagingly of MTV.

Works Cited

Arac, Jonathan. 1986. *Postmodernism and Politics*. Minneapolis: University of Minnesota Press.

Awkward, Michael. 1989. *Inspiriting Influences: Tradition, Revision and Afro-American Women's Novel*. New York: Columbia University Press.

Baker, Houston. 1990a. "Practical Philosophy and Vernacular Openings: The Poetry Project and the American Mind." Unpublished paper.

———. 1990b. "Handling 'Crisis': Great Books, Rap Music, and the End of Western Homogeneity (Reflections on the Humanities in America)." *Callaloo* 13, no. 2: 173–94.

———. 1993. *Black Studies: Rap and the Academy*. Chicago: University of Chicago Press.

Banes, Ruth A. 1992. "Dixie's Daughters: The Country Music Female." In *You Wrote My Life: Lyrical Themes in Country Music*, edited by Melton A. McLaurin and Richard A. Peterson. Philadelphia: Gordon and Breach.

Barreca, Regina, ed. 1988. *Last Laughs: Perspectives on Women and Comedy*. New York: Gordon and Breach.

———. 1991. *They Used to Call Me Snow White . . . But I Drifted*. New York: Viking.

Baudrillard, Jean. 1989. *America*. Translated by Chris Turner. New York: Verso.

———. 1990. *Seduction*. Translated by Brian Singer. New York: St. Martin's Press.

Bego, Mark. 1992. *Madonna: Blonde Ambition*. New York: Harmony Books.

Benhabib, Seyla. 1992. *Situating the Self: Gender, Community and Postmodernism in Contemporary Ethics*. New York: Routledge.

Bennett, Lerone, Jr. 1968. *Pioneers in Protest*. Chicago: Johnson Publishing Company.

Bogin, Ruth. 1976. *Black Women in Nineteenth-Century American Life*. University Park: Pennsylvania State University Press.

Breitbart, Eric. 1986. "Agit Rock Video: Music TV Goes Political." *Sightlines* 19 (spring/summer): 25.

Brenkman, Jonathan. 1987. *Culture and Domination*. Ithaca: Cornell University Press.

Brown, Jane D., Kenneth Campbell, and Lynn Fischer. 1986. "American Adolescents and Music Videos: Why Do They Watch?" *Gazette* 37: 94–106.

Bufwack, Mary A., and Robert K. Oermann. 1993. *Finding Her Voice: The Saga of Women in Country Music*. New York: Crown.

Butler, Judith. 1990. *Gender Trouble: Feminism and the Subversion of Identity*. New York: Routledge.

Butler, Judith, and Joan W. Scott, eds. 1992. *Feminists Theorize the Politicial*. New York: Routledge.

Carter, Angela. 1987. *Fireworks: Nine Profane Pieces*. New York: Penguin.

Chambers, Gordon, and Joan Morgan. 1992. "Droppin' Knowledge: A Rap Roundtable." *Essence* 23, no. 5 (September): 83–85, 116–18.

Chambers, Iain. 1986. *Popular Culture: The Metropolitan Experience*. New York: Methuen.

Ching, Barbara. 1993. "Acting Naturally: Cultural Distinction and Critiques of Pure Country." *Arizona Quarterly* 49, no. 3 (autumn): 107–25.

Christian, Barbara. 1986. *Black Feminist Criticism: Perspectives on Black Women Writers*. New York: Pergamon.

Cixous, Hélène. 1981. "The Laugh of the Medusa." In *New French Feminisms*, edited by Elaine Marks and Isabelle de Courtivron. New York: Schocken.

Combahee River Collective. 1982. "A Black Feminist Statement." In *All the Women are White, All the Blacks are Men, But Some of Us are Brave*, edited by Gloria T. Hull, Patricia Bell Scott, and Barbara Smith. Old Westbury: Feminist Press.

Connor, Steven. 1989. *Postmodernist Culture: An Introduction to Theories of the Contemporary*. New York: Basil Blackwell.

Costello, Mark, and David Foster Wallace. 1990. *Signifying Rappers: Rap and Race in the Urban Present*. New York: Ecco.

Cusic, Don. 1993. "Comedy and Humor in Country Music." *Journal of American Culture* 16, no. 2 (summer): 45–50.

Dafoe, Chris. 1990. "Rapping Latifah Rules New Tribes." *Toronto Star* (18 May): D8.

Darling, Lynn. 1994. "Speaking the Unspoken." *Harper's Bazaar* (March): 176.

Davis, Angela. 1989. *Women, Culture, and Politics*. New York: Random House.

Denisoff, R. Serge. 1988. *Inside MTV*. New Brunswick: Transaction Books.

Derrida, Jacques. 1977. "Signature Event Context." *Glyph* 1: 172–97.

Diamond, Irene, and Lee Quinby, eds. 1988. *Feminism and Foucault: Reflections on Resistance*. Boston: Northeastern University Press.

Di Stefano, Christine. 1990. "Dilemmas of Difference: Feminism, Modernity, and Postmodernism." In *Feminism/Postmodernism*, edited by Linda J. Nicholson. New York: Routledge.

Docker, John. 1994. *Postmodernism and Popular Culture: A Cultural History*. New York: Cambridge University Press.

Ebony. 1990. "Girl Groups Are Back!" 45 (September): 96, 98–100.

Echols, Alice. 1984. "The Taming of the Id: Feminist Sexual Politics, 1968–83." In *Pleasure and Danger: Exploring Female Sexuality*, edited by Carole S. Vance. Boston: Routledge and Kegan Paul.

Ellis, Kate, Nan D. Hunter, Beth Jaker, Barbara O'Dair, and Abby Talmer, eds. 1986. *Caught Looking: Feminism, Pornography, and Censorship*. New York: Caught Looking, Inc.

Epstein, Jonathon S., ed. 1994. *Adolescents and Their Music*. New York: Garland.

Ewen, Stuart. 1988. *All Consuming Images: The Politics of Style in Contemporary Culture*. New York: Basic Books.

Fenster, Mark. 1993. "Genre and Form: The Development of the Country Music Video." In *Sound and Vision: The Music Video Reader*, edited by Simon Frith, Andrew Goodwin, and Lawrence Grossberg. New York: Routledge.

Fiske, John. 1989. *Reading the Popular*. Boston: Unwin Hyman.

Flax, Jane. 1990. "Postmodernism and Gender Relations in Feminist Theory." In *Feminism/Postmodernism*, edited by Linda J. Nicholson. New York: Routledge.

———. 1992. "The End of Innocence." In *Feminists Theorize the Political*, edited by Judith Butler and Joan W. Scott. New York: Routledge.

Foucault, Michel. 1976. *The History of Sexuality*. Vol.1. Translated by Robert Hurley. New York: Vintage.

———. 1989. "What Is an Author?" In *Contemporary Literary Criticism*, edited by Robert Con Davis and Ronald Schleifer. New York: Longman.

Frith, Simon.1981. *Sound Effects*. New York: Pantheon.

———. 1988. *Music for Pleasure: Essays in the Sociology of Pop*. New York: Polity.

Gaar, Gillian G. 1992. *She's a Rebel: The History of Women in Rock and Roll*. Seattle: Seal Press.

George, Nelson. 1989. "Rap's 10th Birthday." *Village Voice* 24, no. 43 (24 October): 40.

Giddings, Paula. 1988. *When and Where I Enter: The Impact of Black Women on Race and Sex in America*. New York: Bantam.

Gilbert, Sandra M., and Susan Gubar. 1979. *The Madwoman in the Attic*. New Haven: Yale University Press.

———. 1986. "The Queen's Looking Glass." In *Don't Bet on the Prince*, edited by Jack Zipes. New York: Methuen.

Goldstein, Richard. 1990. "Free MTV!" *Village Voice* (18 December): 52.

Goodwin, Andrew. 1992. *Dancing in the Distraction Factory: Music Television and Popular Culture*. Minneapolis: University of Minnesota Press.

Gordon, Linda, and Ellen DuBois. 1987. "Seeking Ecstasy on the Battlefield: Danger and Pleasure in Nineteenth-Century Feminist Social Thought." In *Sexuality: A Reader*, edited by *Feminist Review*. London: Virago.

Greenfield, Jeff. 1993. ABC News, 30 July.

Grossberg, Lawrence. 1984. " 'I'd Rather Feel Bad Than Not Feel Anything At All': Rock and Roll, Pleasure and Power." *enclitic* 8 (spring/fall): 94–111.

Harper's Bazaar. 1994. "Music" (March): 178.

Harrison, Daphne Duval. 1988. *Black Pearls: Blues Queens of the 1920s.* New Brunswick: Rutgers University Press.

Hebdige, Dick. 1987. *Cut 'n Mix.* New York: Methuen.

Hine, Darlene Clark, ed. 1993. *Black Women in America.* Vol. 2. Brooklyn: Carlson Publishing.

Holly, Susan. 1993. "A Country Twist at Every Turn." *Nation's Business* 81 (March): 33–34, 36, 37.

hooks, bell. 1989. *Talking Back: Thinking Feminist, Thinking Black.* Boston: South End Press.

Howell, John. 1993. "Country Divas." *Mademoiselle* 99 (October): 108.

Hull, Gloria T., Patricia Bell Scott, and Barbara Smith. 1982. *But Some of Us Are Brave: Black Women's Studies.* New York: Feminist Press.

Jameson, Frederic. 1988. "Postmodernism and Consumer Society." In *Postmodernism and Its Discontents*, edited by E. Ann Kaplan. New York: Verso.

————. 1991. *Postmodernism, or, The Cultural Logic of Late Capitalism.* Durham: Duke University Press.

Janowitz, Tama. 1987. "Sex as a Weapon." *Spin* 3, no. 1: 54.

Jhally, Sut. 1991. *Dreamworlds.* Videocassette.

Kaplan, E. Ann. 1985. "A Post-Modern Play of the Signifier? Advertising, Pastiche and Schizophrenia in Music Television." In *Television in Transition*, edited by Phillip Drummond and Richard Patterson. London: British Film Institute.

————. 1987. *Rocking Around the Clock: Music Television, Postmodernism and Consumer Culture.* New York: Methuen.

————. 1988. "Feminism / Oedipus / Postmodernism: The

Case of MTV." In *Postmodernism and Its Discontents: Theories, Practices,* edited by E. Ann Kaplan. New York: Verso.

————, ed. 1988. *Postmodernism and Its Discontents: Theories, Practices.* New York: Verso.

Karlen, Neal. 1994. *Babes in Toyland: The Making and The Selling of a Rock and Roll Band.* New York: Random House.

Kennedy, Dana. 1991. "Female Rappers Earn Big Money and Respect For Women." *Sunday Republican* (13 January): E10.

Keyes, Cheryl L. 1993. " 'We're More than a Novelty, Boys': Strategies of Female Rappers in the Rap Music Tradition." In *Feminist Messages: Coding in Women's Folk Culture,* edited by Joan Newlon Radner. Urbana: University of Illinois Press.

Kinder, Marsha. 1984. "Music Video and the Spectator: Television, Ideology and Dream." *Film Quarterly* 38 (fall): 2–15.

Kingsbury, Paul. 1992a. "Interview: Trisha Yearwood Gets Serious." *Journal of Country Music* 15, no. 1: 12–19.

————. 1992b. "Will the Circle Be Unbroken: Threads of an Ongoing Conversation." *Journal of Country Music* 15, no. 1: 28–30.

————. 1992c. "Women Walk the Line." *Journal of Country Music* 15, no. 1: 20–35.

Kort, Michelle. 1985. "Homecoming Queen Number One with a Bullet." *Ms.* 13 (October): 60.

Kosser, Mike. 1994. *Hot Country Women.* New York: Avon.

Lakoff, Robin. 1973. "Language and Women's Place." *Language and Society* 2: 45–79.

Lazere, Donald, ed. 1987. *American Media and Mass Culture.* Berkeley: University of California Press.

Lee, Tanith. 1983. *Red as Blood or Tales from the Sisters Grimmer.* New York: DAW.

Leland, John. 1994. "Our Bodies, Our Sales." *Newsweek* (31 January): 56–57.

Lelyvald, Joseph. 1985. *Move Your Shadow: South Africa, Black and White.* New York: Times Books.

Leonard, John. 1993. "TV and the Decline of Civilization." *Nation* (27 December): 785–801, 802–4.

Lewis, Lisa A. 1990. *Gender Politics and MTV: Voicing the Difference.* Philadelphia: Temple University Press.

———, ed. 1992. *Adoring Audience: Fan Culture and Popular Media.* New York: Routledge.

Linden, Amy. 1994. "Me'shell NdegeOcello: Hip-hop Song Stylist." *Essence* 24 (January):36.

Loewenberg, Bert James, and Ruth Bogin, eds. 1976. *Black Women in Nineteenth-Century Life.* University Park: Pennsylvania State University Press.

Lorde, Audre. 1984. "Uses of the Erotic: The Erotic as Power." In *Sister/Outsider: Essays and Speeches.* Trumansburg, NY: Crossing Press.

Lyotard, Jean-François. 1984. *The Postmodern Condition: A Report on Knowledge.* Translated by Geoff Bennington and Brian Massumi. Minneapolis: University of Minnesota Press.

Malone, Bill. 1985. *Country Music, U.S.A.* Austin: University of Texas Press.

Marcuse, Herbert. 1965. "Repressive Tolerance." In *A Critique of Pure Tolerance.* Boston: Beacon.

Mayfield, G. 1990. "Retail Track: Still-small Presence of Women and Blacks in the Sales and Distribution Networks of Major Music Companies." *Billboard* 102: 40–41.

McDonnell, Evelyn. 1989. "New Music Seminar Forum Stirs Angry Audience Reaction." *Billboard* 101: 30.

———. 1991. "Me'shell NdegeOcello." *Village Voice* (1 January): 32–33.

McLaurin, Melton A. 1992. "Songs of the South: The Changing Image of the South in Country Music." In *You Wrote My Life: Lyrical Themes in Country Music,* edited by Melton A. McLaurin and Richard A. Peterson. Philadelphia: Gordon and Breach.

McRobbie, Angela. 1994. *Postmodernism and Popular Culture.* New York: Routledge.

Meisler, Andy. 1994. "The Ever-Expanding Realm of Queen Latifah." *New York Times* (9 January): 29, 33.

Mohan, Amy B., and Jean Malone. 1994. "Popular Music as a 'Social Cement': A Content Analysis of Social Criticism and Alienation in Alternative Music Song Titles." In *Adolescents and Their Music*, edited by Jonathan S. Epstein. New York: Garland Publishing, Inc.

Morgan, Joan. 1991. "Throw the 'F.' " *Village Voice* (11 June): 75.

Morgan, Robin. 1987. *Dry Your Smile*. New York: Doubleday.

"Much Music." 1990. Toronto, Canada. 19 May. Television program.

Mulvey, Laura. 1989. *Visual and Other Pleasures*. Bloomington: Indiana University Press.

Natoli, Joseph, and Linda Hutcheon, eds. 1993. *A Postmodernism Reader*. Albany: SUNY Press.

Nicholson, Linda, ed. 1990. *Feminism/Postmodernism*. New York: Routledge.

Painton, Priscilla. 1992. *Time* 139 (30 March): 62–66.

Pareles, Jon. 1990. "How Rap Moves to Television's Beat." *New York Times* (14 January): 2: 1.

Parsons, Patrick R. 1988. "The Changing Role of Women Executives in the Recording Industry." *Popular Music and Society* 12: 31–42.

Pepe, Barbara. 1986. "Annie Lennox of the 'Eurythmics': Would She Lie to You?" *Ms.* 14, no. 8 (February): 12, 14, 16.

Princenthal, Nancy. 1989. "Jenny Holzer's 'Laments' at Dia: The Quick and the Dead." *Village Voice* (14 March): 31–32.

Radner, Joan Newlon, ed. 1993. *Feminist Messages: Coding in Women's Folk Culture*. Urbana: University of Illinois Press.

Radner, Joan Newlon, and Susan S. Lanser. 1993. "Strategies of Coding in Women's Cultures." In *Feminist Messages: Coding in Women's Folk Culture*, edited by Joan Newlon Radner. Urbana: University of Illinois Press.

Rap City. 1990. Black Entertainment Television. 7 July.

Rich, B. Ruby. 1986. "Review Essay: Feminism and Sexuality in the 1980s." *Feminist Studies* 12: 525–61.

Ritz, David. 1993. "Janet Jackson Finds Peace, Inspiration, and Chart Success Through Carnal Knowledge." *Rolling Stone* 665 (16 September): 39–43, 82.

Roberts, Robin. 1991. "Music Videos, Performance and Resistance: Feminist Rappers." *Journal of Popular Culture* 25: 141–52.

———. 1993. *A New Species: Gender and Science in Science Fiction.* Urbana: University of Illinois Press.

Robinson, Wilhelmena S. 1967. *Historical Negro Biographies.* New York: Publishers Company.

Rogers, Jimmie N. 1989. *The Country Music Message: Revisited.* Fayetteville: University of Arkansas Press.

Rose, Jacqueline. 1986. *Sexuality in the Field of Vision.* New York: Verso.

Rose, Tricia. 1990. "One Queen, One Tribe, One Destiny." *Village Voice.* 3, no. 1 (spring): 10–11, 16, 19.

———. 1991. "Never Trust A Big Butt and a Smile." *Camera Obscura* 23: 108–31.

———. 1994. *Black Noise: Rap Music and Black Culture in Contemporary America.* Hanover: University Press of New England.

Rusche, Sue. 1988. Column, *The Morning Advocate* (1 December): 2C.

Saloy, Mona Lisa. 1990. "The Tradition Continues: Shining in New Orleans." *Meschabe:* 15–21.

Sapiro, Virginia. 1986. *Women in American Society.* Palo Alto: Mayfield.

Sawicki, Jana. 1991. *Disciplining Foucault: Feminism, Power, and the Body.* New York: Routledge.

Schoemer, Karen. 1993. "No Hair Spray No Spangles." *The New York Times Magazine* (August): 36–37, 44, 47.

Sessums, Kevin. 1995. "Love Story: The Long, Strange Trip of Rock Icon Courtney Love." *Vanity Fair* (June): 106–15.

Shales, Tom. 1993. "Leave It to Beavis." *The Washington Post, National Weekly Edition* 10, no. 51 (18–24 October): 8–9.

Singer, Linda. 1992. "Feminism and Postmodernism." In *Feminists Theorize the Political*, edited by Judith Butler and Joan W. Scott. New York: Routledge.

Spencer, Jon Michael, ed. 1991. *The Emergency of Black and the Emergence of Rap*. Durham: Duke University Press.

Spillers, Hortense. 1984. "Interstices: A Small Drama of Words." In *Pleasure and Danger: Exploring Female Sexuality*, edited by Carole S. Vance. Boston: Routledge and Kegan Paul.

Teachout, Terry. 1990. "Rap and Racism." *Commentary* (March): 60.

Texier, Catherine. 1990. "Have Women Surrendered in MTV's Battle of the Sexes?" *New York Times* (22 April): 29.

Tichi, Cecelia. 1994. *High Lonesome: The American Culture of Country Music*. Chapel Hill: University of North Carolina Press.

Toop, David. 1984. *The Rap Attack: African Jive to New York Hip Hop*. Boston: South End Press.

———. 1992. *Rap Attack 2: African Rap to Global Hip Hop*. New York: Serpent's Tail.

Vance, Carole S., ed. 1984. *Pleasure and Danger: Exploring Female Sexuality*. Boston: Routledge and Kegan Paul.

Walker, Nancy. 1988. *A Very Serious Thing: Women's Humor and American Culture*. Minneapolis: University of Minnesota Press.

Wallace, Michelle. 1990a. *Invisibility Blues: From Pop to Theory*. New York: Verso.

———. 1990b. "When Black Feminism Faces the Music and the Music is Rap." *New York Times* (29 July): C11–12.

Walters, Barry. 1987. *Village Voice* (2 June): 40.

Waugh, Patricia, ed. 1992. *Postmodernism: A Reader*. New York: Edward Arnold.

Weedon, Chris. 1987. *Feminist Practice and Poststructuralist Theory*. London: Basil Blackwell.

Weinstein, Deena. 1994. "Expendable Youth: The Rise and Fall of Youth Culture." In *Adolescents and Their Music*, edited by Jonathan Epstein. New York: Garland Publishing Inc.

West, Cornel. 1989. "Black Culture and Postmodernism." In *Remaking History*, edited by Barbara Kruger and Phil Mariani. Seattle: Bay Press.

Williams, Linda. 1989. *Hard Core: Power, Pleasure, and the Frenzy of the Visible*. Berkeley: University of California Press.

Willis, Ellen. 1983. "Feminism, Moralism, and Pornography." In *Powers of Desire: The Politics of Sexuality*, edited by Ann Snitow, Christine Stansell, and Sharon Thompson. New York: Monthly Review Press.

———. 1992a. "Nature's Revenge." In *No More Nice Girls: Counter-Culture Essays*. Hanover: University Press of New England.

———. 1992b. Introduction to *Beginning to See the Light: Sex, Hope, and Rock-and-Roll*. Hanover: University Press of New England.

Wolff, Janet. 1990. *Feminine Sentences: Essays on Women and Culture*. Berkeley: University of California Press.

Young, Charles. 1994. "Meet the Beavis: The Last Word from America's Phenomenal Pop Combo." *Rolling Stone* 678: 38–39, 42.

Zipes, Jack, ed. 1986. *Don't Bet on the Prince: Contemporary Feminist Fairy Tales in North America and England*. New York: Methuen.

Videography

Brown, Julie. 1985. *Comedy Videos*. Stamford, CT: Vestron Video, VA3120.

En Vogue. *Funky Divas*. 1992. New York: Atlantic Recording Co., 50326-3.

Jackson, Janet. 1986. *Control: The Videos*. Hollywood: A & M Video, VC 61101.

Lennox, Annie. 1992. *Diva*. New York: BMG Video, 07822-15719-3.

Lyte, M. C. 1990. *Rap from Atlantic St., Vol. 1*. New York: Atlantic Video, 501443.

Madonna. *Justify My Love*. 1990. New York: Warner Reprise, 38224-3.

Sisters in the Name of Rap. 1991. New York: Polygram Video, 084495-3.

Index

Abdul, Paula, 140

Adam and Eve, 19

"Addicted to Love" (Palmer), 66

Adoring Audience: Fan Culture and Popular Media, The (Lewis), 61

Advertising, 24; and negative images of women, 18, 19–21, 31, 65, 103, 108, 169

African National Congress, 166, 176–77, 178

Afrocentricity, 164–68, 170–73, 181, 182–83

Ain't I a Woman (hooks), 175

All Hail the Queen (Queen Latifah), 164

Allen, Deborah, 127

Alternative music, 81–92

Alternative Nation, 92, 103

American Family Association, 60

Androgyny, in female performers, 25–26

Antoinette, 140, 169, 170, 180

Appropriation, of African-American music and culture, 50, 51, 52, 167

Arac, Jonathan, 11

Atkins, Chet, 114

Authorship, multiple, 12; in music videos, 9, 12, 16–17, 27, 117–18

Awkward, Michael, 170

B-52s, 56

Babcock, Barbara, 122

Babes in Toyland, 82, 83, 88, 91–92, 96–98, 104

Baker, Houston, 167

Bambatta, Afrika, 152

Barbin, Herbert, 101

Barnes, Dee, 153, 154, 158

Barreca, Regina, 32, 34–35, 44

Baudrillard, Jean, 10, 14, 52, 62

Beauty pageant contestants, 16, 40, 89–91, 107

Beauvoir, Simone de, 88
Beavis and Butt-Head, 34, 45, 53, 56, 57, 92–109
Bego, Mark, 77
Benatar, Pat, 18–21, 24, 28, 31, 34, 51, 65
Benhabib, Seyla, 8, 23
Bernhard, Sandra, 78–79
BET. *See* Black Entertainment Television
"Bikini Girls with Machine Guns" (Cramps), 104, 106–08
Bjelland, Kat, 88, 97–98
Black Entertainment Television (BET), 17, 140–41, 153, 168, 169
"Black Feminist Statement, A," 170
Black Noise: Rap Music and Black Culture in Contemporary America
    (Rose), 139–40
Blues singers, 67–68, 144, 148
Bogguss, Suzy, 119, 124–27, 130, 132, 135
Bond, James, 19, 179
Bowie, David, 34
Bozio, Dale, 21
"Break These Chains" (Allen), 127
Breitbart, Eric, 18
Brown, James, 165
Brown, Julie, 34, 35–36, 37–46, 53, 54, 55, 56, 58, 77, 87, 91,
    107, 126–27, 183
"Bruise Violet" (Babes in Toyland), 97, 104
Bufwack, Mary, 112–13, 116
"Burning Bed, The," 129
Butthole Surfers, 104, 106
Buzz Clips, 92

"California Girls" (Roth), 47, 66
Carpenter, Mary-Chapin, 127, 131, 132, 134–35
Carrie (King), 43
Carter, Angela, 41
Caught Looking, 64
Censorship, 37, 60, 77
Cherry, Neneh, 140
Ching, Barbara, 115
Christian, Barbara, 144
Cinderella figure, 16, 38, 40, 41, 119, 124–27

Citizen Kane, 38
Cixous, Hélène, 45
Cleopatra figures, 16, 122, 148, 149
"Cleopatra, Queen of Denial" (Tillis), 119, 121–24, 135, 148
Cline, Patsy, 132
Clinton, Hillary Rodham, 112
CMT. *See* Country Music Television
Cobain, Kurt, 88
Coffey, Charlie, 39, 46
Colby College, 71
Combahee River Collective, 170
Communist Party, 175
"Company Time" (Davis), 127
Connor, Steven, 12
Control (Jackson), 22, 67
Cops, 106
Country music, 110–37, 139
Country Music Award, 127
Country Music Television (CMT), 17, 113, 126
Country Music, U.S.A. (Malone), 116–17
Cramps, 104, 106–08
Cusic, Don, 120–21
"Cuz I'm a Blond" (Brown), 45
Cycle Sluts from Hell, 104–05

Dalton, Lacy J., 133
Dance, 23–24, 25, 65, 73, 150–51, 155, 157, 179–80
Davis, Angela, 143, 165, 171, 172, 173, 175–76, 177, 180
Davis, Linda, 127
Deconstruction, 12–13
Derrida, Jacques, 13, 27
Di Stephano, Christine, 8
Disney, Walt, 41
Diva (Lennox), 26–29
"Do You Really Want Me?" (Salt 'n Pepa), 157
Docker, John, 12
Domestic violence, 119, 127–30, 184
Dreamworlds, 61, 93
Dunn, Susan, 134

Dutcheez, 154
Dworkin, Andrea, 64

Earth Girls Are Easy, 45
East Orange (N.J.), 165
Ellis, Terry, 70, 71, 73, 76
En Vogue, 59–60, 69–76, 79–80, 99–100
"Erotic as Power, The" (Lorde), 68
Estep, Maggie, 35, 36, 37, 53–55, 56, 98–99
Eurythmics, 25, 29
"Every Dog Has His Day" (Wallace), 144
"Everything We Got We Got the Hard Way," 135
"Express Yourself" (Madonna), 77

Fabio, 57, 67
Fad, J. J., 140
Fairy tales, 124–27
Feminine Endings: Music, Gender and Sexuality (McClary), 77
Femininity, construction of, 14, 28–31, 38, 40, 43, 44, 56, 75,
     76–77, 83, 84–85, 91, 92, 97–98, 122–23
Feminism/Postmodernism (Nicholson), 4, 7–8
Feminist Practice and Poststructuralist Theory (Weedon), 4, 6
Fenster, Mark, 130, 137
Fiedler, Leslie, 9, 10
Finding Her Voice: The Saga of Women in Country Music (Bufwack
     and Oermann), 112–13
Flax, Jane, 5–6
"Fly Girl" (Queen Latifah), 159
Forester Sisters, 133–34
Foucault, Michel, 7, 13, 27–28, 101
Fox Television, 46, 153, 183
Fragmentation, 14–15, 18, 20, 21, 28, 34, 47, 49–50, 67, 79, 82,
     86, 91, 96, 104, 111, 125, 126, 143, 164, 167
Frankfurt School, 95
Franklin, Aretha, 25–26, 72, 163, 165
"Free Your Mind" (En Vogue), 75–76
Frith, Simon, 112, 142
Funky Divas (En Vogue), 70, 72

Gaar, Gillian, 82

Gangsta rap, 146

Gender Politics and MTV (Lewis), 61, 103

Gender roles, 8–9, 14–15, 18–20, 28–29, 31, 35–36, 37, 39, 40–44, 45, 46–47, 50, 51, 54, 66, 79, 85–86, 89, 92, 98, 100–01, 104–05, 121–22, 124

Genres, breakdown of, 15, 18, 20, 21, 33, 34, 36, 39, 50, 82, 92, 164

George, Nelson, 144–45

Get Smart, 179

Giddings, Paula, 174

"Gift, The" (Lennox), 26

Gilbert, Sandra, 41

"Giving Him Something He Can Feel" (En Vogue), 74–75

Glas (Derrida), 27

"God Bless Texas," 117

Goldberg, Danny, 87–88

Goldstein, Richard, 77–78, 79

Goodwin, Andrew, 61–62, 65

Gore, Tipper, 60

Grand Daddy IU, 155

Grand Ole Opry, 120

Gubar, Susan, 41

"Hangin' In" (Tucker), 123

Harris, Emmylou, 132, 135

Harrison, Daphne Duval, 144

Hassan, Ihab, 12

"He Thinks He'll Keep Her" (Carpenter), 127, 132, 134–35

Heavy metal, 104

Hebdige, Dick, 143, 165

Herron, Cindy, 71

"Heterosexual Man" (Odds), 104, 105

"Hey Baby" (Estep), 35, 37, 53–55, 98–99

"Hey Cinderella" (Bogguss), 119, 124–47

High Lonesome (Tichi), 113

Hip Hop. *See* Rap music

Hole, 82, 83, 87–92

Holly, Susan, 111

Holzer, Jenny, 19
"Homecoming Queen's Got a Gun, The" (Brown), 35–36, 37–45, 50, 54, 77, 87, 91, 107, 123, 126–27
hooks, bell, 175
Hot Country Women (Kosser), 118–19
Howe, Irving, 9, 13
Humor, 15–16, 20, 24, 32–58, 87, 92–109, 119, 120–22, 123–24
Hurston, Zora Neale, 171
Hutcheon, Linda, 10, 12

"I Believe in Me" (Nicole), 154
"I Kissed a Girl" (Sobule), 35, 37, 55, 66, 169
"I Love Rock 'n' Roll" (Jett), 65
"I Wish You Were a Beer" (Cycle Sluts from Hell), 104–05
Ice Cream Tee, 180
Idol, Billy, 34
"If That's Your Boyfriend" (NdegeOcello), 84–87
"I'm Not Having It" (Lyte), 65
"Independence Day" (McBride), 85, 119, 127–30
Intelligent Black Woman's Coalition (IBWC), 155
Intertextuality, in music videos, 25
"Into the Groove" (Madonna), 65
Irigaray, Luce, 122
Isley Brothers, 150
"It's a Little Too Late" (Tucker), 135
"It's Your Thing" (Isley Brothers), 150, 152

Jackson, Janet, 17, 21–25, 28, 31, 67–68, 72
Jackson, Michael, 23
Jameson, Frederic, 13, 14, 33–34
Jett, Joan, 65
Jhally, Sut, 61, 62, 63, 93, 105
"Johnny Angel," 43
Johnson, Simone. See Love, Monie
Jones, Grace, 148, 149
Jones, Maxine, 71, 72, 73
Judge, Mike, 108–09
Just Say Julie, 45
"Justify My Love" (Madonna), 69, 77–79

Karlen, Neal, 97

Kaufman, Gloria, 33

"Keep Young and Beautiful" (Lennox), 26

Keyes, Cheryl L., 141–42

King, Stephen, 43

Kingsbury, Paul, 111–12

Kosser, Mike, 118–19

Kristeva, Julia, 86

Kruger, Barbara, 19

L-7, 83

"L. A. Law," 66

Lacan, Jacques, 13, 86

"Ladies First" (Queen Latifah), 158–59, 160, 162, 163–64, 167, 168, 170, 171–84

Lakoff, Robin, 179

Language, as gendered system, 86

Lanser, Susan, 113, 122

Las Vegas, 50–52

Last Laughs: Perspectives on Women and Comedy (Barreca), 32

"Laugh of the Medusa, The" (Cixous), 45

Lauper, Cyndi, 34

"Leader of the Pack, The," 43

Lee, Tanith, 41

Leland, John, 59–60

Lennox, Annie, 25–31, 34, 70, 72, 74, 84, 107, 127, 163

Lesbianism, 55–58, 66–67, 78–79

"Let's Talk About Sex" (Salt 'n Pepa), 65, 157

Lewis, Lisa A., 10, 61, 65, 103

Lincoln, Abraham, 175

Live Through This (Hole), 83, 88–89

"Living Single," 183, 184

Loder, Kurt, 88

Lollapalooza Festival, 82, 83

Longacre, Susan, 132

Lorde, Audre, 68, 156

Los Angeles, 156

Love, Courtney, 83, 87–92, 109

Love, Monie (Simone Johnson), 164, 170, 171, 172, 178–79, 180–82
"Love American Style," 43
"Love Is a Battlefield" (Benatar), 65
Loveless, Patty, 127, 131, 132, 135
Lynn, Loretta, 114, 115, 116, 131, 132
Lyotard, Jean-François, 5, 82–83
Lyte, M. C., 65, 138, 140, 145–49, 161, 168
"Lyte as a Rock" (Lyte), 145–49

McBride, Martina, 119, 127–30, 133
McClary, Susan, 77
McEntire, Reba, 123
MacKinnon, Catherine, 64
McRobbie, Angela, 4, 6, 8, 10–11, 14
Maddox, Rose, 131
Madonna, 45, 65, 69, 71, 76–80, 83, 87, 156
Madonna: Blonde Ambition (Bego), 77
Malcolm X, 146, 147, 149
Malone, Bill, 116–17
Malone, Jean, 81, 82
Mandela, Winnie, 171, 176–77
Mann, Aimee, 44
Mapplethorpe, Robert, 60
Marcuse, Herbert, 14, 93
Martin, Jerry, 119
Marxists, 61, 62
Massachusetts, University of, 61
Master narratives, critique of, 82–83, 111, 119
Mattea, Kathy, 132
Maverick (record label), 83
Medusa: Dare to Be Truthful, 45
Mellencamp, John, 83
"Men" (Forester Sisters), 133–34
Milwaukee, 71
"Miss World" (Hole), 87, 88–91
"Missing Persons," 21
Mohan, Amy B., 81, 82
Monroe, Marilyn, 19, 87

Montage, 14
Montana, Patsy, 131
Morgan, Lorrie, 132, 135
Morgan, Robin, 41
"Most Men Are Tramps" (Salt 'n Pepa), 156–57
Motown Records, 183
Ms. Melodie, 138, 140, 180
MTV. *See* Music Television
MTV Jams, 140
MTV Music Video Awards, 70, 71
Mulvey, Laura, 69, 101
Music Television (MTV), 17, 18, 34, 37, 45, 46, 53, 55, 59, 61–
    62, 77, 78, 83, 88, 89, 92–109, 126, 140–41, 149, 152, 160,
    168–69

Nashville, 114, 116, 120
Nashville Network, The (TNN), 17, 113, 118, 127
"Nasty" (Jackson), 21–25, 31, 67–68
National Endowment for the Arts, 60
National Negro Business League Convention, 174
National Women's Suffrage Convention, 174–75
Natoli, Joseph, 10, 12
NdegeOcello, Me'shell, 83–87, 91, 109
"Never Trust a Big Butt and a Smile" (Rose), 138–39
New Species: Gender and Science in Science Fiction, A (Roberts),
    13
New York Times, 37
Nicholson, Linda J., 4, 6, 7–8, 11–12
Nikki Nicole, 154–55, 156
Nirvana, 88
No More Mister Nice Girl, 55
"Now I Know" (White), 127
N.W.A., 161

Odds, 104, 105
Oermann, Robert, 112–13, 116
Oldenburg, Claes, 50
"Open Your Heart" (Madonna), 77
Owens, Dana. *See* Queen Latifah

Palmer, Robert, 66

Pareles, Jon, 142, 169

Parents' Music Resource Center (PMRC), 60, 61, 62, 63, 93, 105

Paris Is Burning, 29

Parody, 91, 92, 106

Parton, Dolly, 120, 123

Pastiche, 18–19, 20, 24, 25, 33, 36, 39, 40, 43, 44, 50, 56, 66, 67, 91, 92, 143, 164

People, 150

Pepe, Barbara, 25–26

Peters, Gretchen, 127

"Picket Fences," 66

Pleasure and Danger: Exploring Female Sexuality (Vance), 64

Positive K, 65

Postmodern Condition, The (Lyotard), 5

Postmodernism and Popular Culture (McRobbie), 4, 8

Precious, 140

Presley, Elvis, 36, 37, 50–52, 53, 135

"Princess of the Posse" (Queen Latifah), 169

Public Enemy, 161

Pump It Up, 153

"Push It" (Salt 'n Pepa), 140, 150

Queen Latifah (Dana Owens), 138, 139, 140, 144, 158–60, 161, 162, 163–84

Racism, 49, 139, 140, 146, 148, 149, 150, 163, 166, 172, 175, 176–78, 182, 183

Radner, Joan, 113, 122

Rap City, 140, 153, 169, 179

Rap music, 11, 51, 84, 110–11, 114, 138–62

Reis, Sally, 71

Rich, Adrienne, 80

Rich, B. Ruby, 32

Riot Grrrls, 97

Rising to the Challenge: A Revealing Look at the Pied Pipers of Today's Rock 'n' Roll, 60–61

Robinson, Dawn, 71, 72

Rock Blocks, 17
Rockvideo Monthly, 82, 92
Rogers, Jimmie, 115
Rolling Stone, 83, 96
Rose, Jacqueline, 63
Rose, Tricia, 138–40, 159, 173, 180
"Roseanne," 66
Roth, David Lee, 47, 66
Roxanne (The Real), 35–36, 50–53, 138, 140, 168
"Roxanne's on a Roll" (Roxanne), 35, 36–37, 50–53
Ru-Paul, 29

Safari Sisters, 171, 179–80
Salt 'n Pepa, 59–60, 65–66, 99–100, 107, 138, 139, 140, 146,
    149–53, 156–58, 159, 160, 161, 168, 178
Sampling, 143
Scratching, in rap music, 142, 143
Seely, Jeanne, 133
Selassie, Haile, 165
Self-reflexivity, 15, 18, 20, 21–22, 24, 25, 33, 34, 36, 39, 48, 67,
    79, 82, 91, 93, 96, 102, 143, 151, 164
"Sex as a Weapon" (Benatar), 18–21, 24, 31, 65
Sexism, 18–21, 24, 25, 42–43, 47, 59–60, 62, 65, 100, 103, 109,
    110, 113, 116, 117, 123, 140, 141, 142, 146, 148, 149, 150,
    152, 153, 161, 163, 166, 172, 175, 176, 177, 182, 184
Sexual harassment, 21–22, 31, 36, 53–55, 98–100, 127, 184
Sexuality, 104; adolescent male, 100–02, 109; female, 16, 19,
    22, 23–24, 46–47, 48–49, 52, 59–80, 106–08, 148, 150, 151,
    156–58
"Shake, Rattle and Roll" (Antoinette), 170
"Shake Your Thang" (Salt 'n Pepa), 150–53
Shakim, 170
Shales, Tom, 93–94
Shante, Roxanne, 140, 155
Shaw, Victoria, 127
Sherman, Cindy, 18, 38, 97
She's a Rebel (Gaar), 82
"Shoop" (Salt 'n Pepa), 65–66, 67, 107, 140
Showtime, 45

Simpson, Bart, 94

Singer, Linda, 4, 6

Singleton, John, 83

Siouxsie and the Banshees, 103

"Sisters Are Doin' It for Themselves" (Lennox and Franklin), 25, 163

"Sisters in the Name of Rap," 130–31, 153–61

Situating the Self: Gender, Community and Postmodernism in Contemporary Ethics (Benhabib), 8

Snow White, 41

Sobule, Jill, 35, 37, 55–58, 66–67

"Something in Red" (Morgan), 135

Sontag, Susan, 10

South Africa, 158, 166, 167, 171, 172, 176–78, 183

Spillers, Hortense, 23, 67–68

Spin, 83

Spoken Word, 53, 98

"Stand by Your Man" (Wynette), 112

Star Wars, 146

Stewart, Dave, 25

"Supersonic" (Fad), 140

Sweet Tee, 140, 169

Sylvia, 133

Tam Tam, 155

Teachout, Terry, 138

"Tears Dry" (Shaw), 127

Thunder, Shelly, 140, 180

Tichi, Cecelia, 111, 113

Tillis, Mel, 120

Tillis, Pam, 115, 119, 120–24, 130, 131, 132–33, 135, 148

TNN. *See* Nashville Network, The

Toast, 84, 144, 165

Tommy Boy Records, 169

Tone Loc, 141

Toop, David, 143

Trouble, MC, 154

Truth, Sojourner, 171, 173, 174–75, 176

Truth or Dare (Madonna), 45

Tubman, Harriet, 171, 172, 173, 177, 178, 180
Tucker, Tanya, 123, 135
Turner, Tina, 34, 35, 36, 37, 46–50, 53, 55, 56, 166
2 Live Crew, 139, 161
"Typical Male" (Turner), 35, 37, 46–50, 55
Tyson, Cicely, 171, 177

"U. N. I. T. Y." (Queen Latifah), 183–84

Vance, Carole S., 64
Vanity Fair, 87–88
VH–1, 17, 96, 118
Video Hit One, 117–18
"Visual Pleasure and Narrative Cinema" (Mulvey), 69

Walker, Alice, 171
Walker, Madam C. J., 171, 173–74, 175, 176
Walker, Nancy, 32, 33, 40, 121
Wallace, Michelle, 138, 161
Wallace, Sippie, 144
Warner Brothers Records, 88, 97
Waugh, Patricia, 13–14
Weedon, Chris, 4, 6–7, 8
West, Cornel, 10–11, 142, 143, 145, 161
West Africa, 174
"What Have You Done for Me Lately" (Jackson), 22, 23
"What Is an Author?" (Foucault), 27–28
"What's Love Got to Do with It?" (Turner), 46
White, Lari, 127
White Zombie, 96
"Who Was in My Room Last Night?" (Butthole Surfers), 104, 106
Who's Zooming Who (Franklin), 25
"Why" (Lennox), 26–31, 74, 84, 107, 126
"Wild Thing" (Tone Loc), 141
Wildmon, Donald, 60
Willis, Ellen, 64, 76–77, 151
Woman Called Moses, A, 171, 177
Women, Culture and Politics (Davis), 176

"Women of Country, The," 116, 119–20, 130–36
Wright, Michelle, 133
Wynette, Tammy, 112, 131, 132, 135

Yankovic, Weird Al, 34
Yearwood, Trisha, 132, 133, 135
Yo MTV Raps, 140, 153, 169
Yo-Yo, 138, 155–56, 158, 160
"You Hurt Me Bad in a Real Good Way" (Loveless), 127, 135
Young, Charles, 96
Young M. C., 152
"You're Never Gonna Get It" (En Vogue), 72–73, 74